Country Cousins: Bigfoot, Mapinguari and the Yowie

Country Cousins: Bigfoot, Mapinguari and the Yowie

Cryptid Comparative Series — Book One

K.M. Graves

Published by K.M. Graves, 2026.

Ebook ISBN: 979-8-9949521-4-6

Paperback ISBN: 979-8-9949521-5-3

Published by K.M. Graves

Table of Contents

Left intentionally blank.

INTRODUCTORY CHAPTERS

In 1938, a fishing trawler working the waters off the coast of South Africa hauled up something that wasn't supposed to exist. Among the day's catch was a large, steel-blue fish with strange lobed fins that moved like stubby legs. The local museum curator, Marjorie Courtenay-Latimer, recognized it as something extraordinary, though she couldn't say exactly what. She contacted a chemistry professor named J.L.B. Smith, who nearly collapsed when he saw it. It was a coelacanth; a fish that every textbook in the world declared had been extinct for sixty-five million years.

The ocean, it turned out, had not read those textbooks.

This is not a book about fish. But it is a book about the distance between what we know and what exists, about the creatures that live in that gap; reported by hundreds, dismissed by institutions, and stubbornly refusing to resolve into either confirmed species or comfortable folklore.

The word for these creatures is *cryptid*, and the study of them is called *cryptozoology*, and both terms carry more baggage than they deserve. Say either word at a university faculty meeting and watch the room shift. Say them at a campfire in the Pacific Northwest, or in a village at the edge of the Amazon basin, or in the Blue Mountains of Australia, and watch the room shift in an entirely different direction. The same words. Different gravity.

This book sits deliberately in the space between those two rooms. It is not a work of advocacy. It will not try to convince you that any particular creature is real in the way that a grizzly bear is real, with a confirmed population count and a page in the field guide. Nor will it treat the subject as an anthropological curiosity, a quaint chapter in the history of human superstition that modern science has outgrown. Both of those approaches are easy, and neither is honest.

What this book will do; what this entire series sets out to do, is take three reported creatures at a time and place them side by side. Not to prove anything, but to see what happens when you do. Because something does happen. Patterns emerge. Consistencies appear where they shouldn't if these accounts were purely imaginary. And inconsistencies appear where they shouldn't if these accounts were straightforwardly true. The picture that develops is more complicated and more interesting than either believers or skeptics tend to allow. In this first volume, the three creatures under examination share a broad family resemblance: they are large, bipedal or semi-bipedal, covered in hair, reported from wilderness areas, and described by witnesses as something like a primate but not quite like any primate we know. They are Bigfoot of North America, the Mapinguari of the Amazon basin, and the Yowie of Australia. Their similarities are striking. Their differences are revealing. And the territory between those two facts is where the real work begins.

Before we get to them, though, we need to establish some shared language. We need to talk about what a cryptid actually is, what cryptozoology is trying to be, and why the comparative method; looking at three rather than one, changes the nature of the questions we can ask.

That starts in the next chapter. For now, it is enough to say this: the map has always had empty spaces. For most of human history, those spaces were simply labeled with honesty, *terra incognita*, unknown land. We have since filled in every coastline, photographed every mountain range from orbit, and threaded GPS signals through the deepest forests on Earth. We are inclined to believe the empty spaces are gone.

The creatures in this book suggest otherwise.

Chapter I: What We Mean When We Say "Cryptid"

The Word Itself

The term *cryptid* is younger than most people assume. It was coined in 1983 by John Wall in a letter to the *International Society of Cryptozoology Newsletter*, and its etymology is straightforward: from the Greek *kryptos*, meaning hidden. A cryptid, in its simplest definition, is an animal whose existence has been suggested but not scientifically confirmed.

That definition is simple, but the category it describes is not. It sprawls. Under the same umbrella, you find the giant squid; a cryptid until 2004, when Japanese researchers finally photographed a living specimen in the deep ocean, and Mokele-mbembe, the alleged living dinosaur of the Congo basin, for which no physical evidence of any kind has ever been produced. You find the mountain gorilla, unknown to Western science until 1902, and you find Mothman, a winged humanoid reported in Point Pleasant, West Virginia, in 1966 and 1967, whose connection to zoology is tenuous at best.

This is the first problem anyone writing seriously about cryptids has to confront: the word covers too much ground. A category that includes both "large ape confirmed to exist after decades of skepticism" and "glowing-eyed flying creature seen before a bridge collapse" is not, on its face, a useful scientific category. It is more like a waiting room; a place where unverified claims sit until they are either promoted to the ranks of known species or quietly escorted out.

And yet the word persists, and the category persists, because it points at something real even if every individual entry in it does not. It points at the fact that our catalog of Earth's species is incomplete, that it has always been incomplete, and that the rate at which we are still discovering new species; particularly large-bodied species in remote habitats, suggests it will remain incomplete for some time.

The Discovery Curve

Consider what the last century has produced. The okapi, a large forest-dwelling relative of the giraffe, was confirmed in 1901. The Komodo dragon, the largest living lizard, was documented by Western science in 1910. The bonobo, one of our closest living relatives, was not recognized as a distinct species until 1929. The megamouth shark, a filter-feeding deep-water species that reaches eighteen feet in length, was not known to science until a specimen was accidentally caught off Hawaii in 1976. The saola, a forest-dwelling bovine in Vietnam and Laos, was discovered in 1992. It weighs roughly two hundred pounds and has horns that can reach twenty inches. It had been living in the Annamite Mountains the entire time.

These are not insects. These are not bacteria. These are large-bodied vertebrates that were unknown to institutional science within living memory. Each of them, before its confirmation, would have qualified as a cryptid; an animal whose existence was suggested (usually by indigenous populations who knew about them perfectly well) but not yet confirmed by the apparatus of formal taxonomy.

This matters because it establishes a precedent. The question is not whether large animals can go undetected by science for extended periods. They demonstrably can. The question is always about the specific case: *this* animal, in *this* habitat, with *this* body of evidence. And that is a question best answered not with broad philosophical arguments about what is possible but with careful attention to what has actually been reported, where, by whom, and under what conditions.

A Working Taxonomy of Cryptids

For the purposes of this series, it helps to sort the vast and unruly world of cryptids into rough categories. These are not formal scientific classifications; nothing in cryptozoology is, but they help clarify what kind of question each type of cryptid poses.

The first category is out-of-place animals: known species reported in locations where they are not supposed to exist. The phantom cats of Britain; large felids reported across the English countryside, fall into this group. The animals themselves are not in doubt. Pumas exist. Leopards exist. The question is whether a viable population of them is living in Surrey.

The second category is surviving relics: species believed to be extinct that may have persisted in isolated habitats. The coelacanth was the most famous member of this group before it was confirmed. The thylacine, or Tasmanian tiger, officially declared extinct in 1936, generates ongoing sighting reports from Tasmania and mainland Australia that place it in this category as well.

The third category is undiscovered species: animals that are entirely new to science. The saola was in this category until 1992. Many of the deep-sea creatures still being discovered fall here. Some cryptids: particularly those reported from biodiversity hotspots in tropical forests, may belong to this group.

The fourth category is the most contentious: animals that challenge existing taxonomic frameworks. These are creatures whose reported characteristics do not map neatly onto any known evolutionary lineage. They are too large, too intelligent, too behaviorally complex, or too anatomically unusual to fit into the phylogenetic trees as we currently understand them. This is the category that generates the most argument, because it sits at the border between zoology and something else; folklore, psychology, or possibly a branch of biology we have not yet developed the tools to pursue.

The three creatures in this book: Bigfoot, Mapinguari, and Yowie, touch multiple categories depending on how you interpret the evidence. That ambiguity is not a weakness. It is, in fact, the point.

What a Cryptid Is Not

A brief clarification, because the boundaries matter. This series treats cryptids as a zoological question, not a paranormal one. There is a tradition within some corners of cryptid research that links these creatures to UFO phenomena, interdimensional travel, psychic communication, or other frameworks that fall outside the scope of biology entirely. That tradition has its own literature and its own logic, and this book does not dismiss the people who pursue it, but it does not follow them.

The operating assumption here is materialist: if these creatures exist, they are biological organisms. They eat, they breed, they occupy ecological niches, they leave physical traces, and they are subject to the same evolutionary pressures as every other living thing. That assumption constrains the discussion, but it also makes the discussion possible, because it allows us to ask questions that have testable answers. Can a population of the reported size sustain itself in the reported habitat? What would its caloric requirements be? What trace evidence should we expect? What does the fossil record suggest about possible lineages?

These are the questions that organize this book. They are scientific questions, even when the subject matter makes the scientific establishment uncomfortable.

Chapter II: The Science of What Might Be There

Cryptozoology's Difficult Name

Cryptozoology has a reputation problem, and it is worth being direct about why.

The field: if it can be called a field, was formalized in the mid-twentieth century, primarily by two men: the Belgian-French zoologist Bernard Heuvelmans and the Scottish-American biologist Ivan T. Sanderson. Heuvelmans published *On the Track of Unknown Animals* in 1955, a work of genuine scholarship that cataloged reports of unidentified creatures from around the world and argued, persuasively, that many of them deserved serious scientific attention. He coined the term *cryptozoology* and spent decades attempting to establish it as a legitimate subdiscipline of zoology.

The problem is that the discipline attracted enthusiasts faster than it attracted rigor. By the 1970s and 1980s, the word *cryptozoology* was attached to television programs, paperback books, and magazine articles that ranged from earnestly investigative to spectacularly credulous. Bigfoot documentaries aired alongside segments about the Bermuda Triangle. Mothman was discussed in the same breath as the Loch Ness Monster, and both were discussed in the same breath as alien abductions. The category blurred. The signal was lost in noise.

This is not a new problem in the history of science; legitimate fields of inquiry have often had to fight their way free from associations with pseudoscience and popular sensationalism, but cryptozoology has never fully managed the escape. Today, it occupies an unusual position: not accepted as a formal scientific discipline by any major academic institution, yet drawing on methods (field observation, track analysis, witness interviews, habitat modeling, genetic sampling) that are individually unimpeachable. The tools are scientific. The institutional framework is not. This creates a credibility gap that has real consequences for the quality of evidence that gets collected, analyzed, and preserved.

What Mainstream Science Has to Offer

Part of the difficulty is that the phenomena cryptozoology investigates do not fit neatly into any existing academic department. A biologist might be the right person to analyze a hair sample or assess the plausibility of a primate population in a given forest. But the same biologist is not necessarily equipped to evaluate the reliability of eyewitness testimony, assess the cultural transmission of sighting narratives, or model the statistical probability of a species avoiding detection over a given period in a given terrain. Those tasks belong to psychologists, anthropologists, and statisticians, respectively. Cryptozoology, when done well, is inherently interdisciplinary. It draws on primatology, ecology, anthropology, psychology, forensic science, and statistical modeling. The problem is that no university has a Department of Cryptozoology, which means no graduate students, no peer-reviewed journal with institutional backing, no systematic training in how to conduct this kind of inquiry properly. The work falls to independent researchers who may be rigorous or may not be, and the public has limited means of distinguishing between them.

This series does not attempt to resolve that structural problem. But it does attempt to demonstrate what the inquiry looks like when it borrows the best practices of multiple disciplines and applies them to specific cases. Each book takes three creatures, examines them through multiple lenses: biological, ecological, cultural, psychological, and asks what picture emerges from the overlap.

The Evidence Spectrum

One of the most common mistakes in discussions about cryptids is treating "evidence" as a binary: either it exists or it doesn't. In practice, evidence for any zoological claim falls along a spectrum, and the position of any given cryptid on that spectrum tells you something important about the nature of the question it poses.

At one end of the spectrum is physical proof: a type specimen, a body, a living capture, DNA from a verified source. This is the standard that formal taxonomy requires, and no cryptid in this book meets it. That fact is not hidden or minimized. It is the central fact of the discussion. At the other end is pure narrative: stories passed through oral tradition with no corroborating physical evidence of any kind. Some cryptids exist only here, and they may be more profitably studied as folklore than as zoology.

In between, however, is a wide and complicated middle ground. This includes trace evidence (footprints, hair samples, scat, tree breaks, nesting structures), photographic and audio evidence (of wildly varying quality), witness testimony (ranging from fleeting glimpses to extended observations by trained professionals), cultural consistency (independent populations reporting similar creatures without apparent contact), and ecological plausibility (habitats capable of supporting the reported organisms).

No single category of evidence in this middle ground is sufficient to confirm a species. But the categories interact. Witness testimony is stronger when it is consistent with trace evidence. Trace evidence is more compelling when the reported habitat could plausibly support the organism. Cultural consistency across populations is harder to explain away when the physical descriptions correlate with ecological conditions. The strength of a cryptid case lies not in any one piece of evidence but in the degree to which independent lines of evidence converge.

This is, incidentally, exactly how many confirmed species were first identified. The mountain gorilla was known from indigenous reports and a few skeletal fragments long before a Western naturalist observed a living specimen. The pattern is not unusual. What is unusual is how reluctant the scientific establishment has been to apply this same evidentiary logic to the cases that remain unconfirmed.

The Modern Landscape

The twenty-first century has changed the terrain of cryptid research in ways that cut in both directions.

On one hand, the tools available for investigation are better than they have ever been. Environmental DNA analysis can detect species from water and soil samples without requiring a physical specimen. Camera trap networks can monitor vast areas of wilderness continuously. Satellite imagery can map habitat with extraordinary precision. Acoustic monitoring can capture and catalog sounds across frequencies that human ears cannot detect. Citizen science platforms allow thousands of observers to contribute data simultaneously. If a large, undiscovered primate were living in any of the habitats discussed in this book, we have more capacity to find evidence of it now than at any point in human history.

On the other hand, the same technological revolution has flooded the field with noise. Digital photography and video editing make fabrication easier and detection of fabrication harder. Social media rewards sensational claims over careful investigation. The line between entertainment and research has become porous in ways that damage credibility. A serious field researcher collecting soil samples in the Pacific Northwest operates in the same information ecosystem as a YouTube channel posting obviously staged encounter videos, and the public often cannot tell the difference.

This tension: better tools and more noise, defines the current moment in cryptid research. Navigating it requires exactly the kind of disciplined, comparative approach this series attempts: not asking "Is Bigfoot real?" as a yes-or-no question, but asking "What does the totality of evidence look like when examined systematically, and what conclusions does that evidence support, resist, or leave open?"

Where This Series Stands

A note on perspective, because the reader deserves to know.

This series is written from a position of informed agnosticism. The author finds the evidence for some cryptids more compelling than the scientific mainstream typically acknowledges, and the evidence for others less compelling than the cryptozoological community often claims. The goal is not to arrive at verdicts but to improve the quality of the questions.

Each volume in this series groups three cryptids that share meaningful characteristics; similar body plans, overlapping behavioral reports, comparable habitats, or parallel cultural contexts. The groupings are deliberate. By placing creatures side by side, we can ask questions that single-creature studies cannot: Why do reports from geographically distant regions describe such similar animals? Why do the differences track so closely with local ecology? What does the pattern of similarities and differences suggest about the possible origin of these reports; whether zoological, psychological, or cultural?

These are not rhetorical questions. They have answers, or at least they have evidence that pushes in identifiable directions. Finding that evidence, examining it honestly, and following it wherever it leads; even when it leads to uncomfortable places for both believers and skeptics, is the work of this series.

Chapter III: Why Three at a Time

The Limits of the Single Case

Most books about cryptids focus on one creature. There are good reasons for this; a single, subject treatment allows for depth, for the full exploration of a sighting history, a cultural context, a body of physical evidence. The literature on Bigfoot alone could fill a small library, and much of it is thorough, well-researched, and valuable. But the single-case approach has a structural weakness: it cannot distinguish between the particular and the general. When you study Bigfoot in isolation, every feature of the phenomenon; the habitat, the behavior, the body type, the pattern of encounters, the quality of evidence, the cultural response, appears unique to Bigfoot. You cannot tell which elements are specific to this creature in this place and which are features of a broader pattern that repeats across continents and cultures.

This matters because patterns are where the real information lives. If a single culture reports a large, hair-covered bipedal creature in its forests, you have a folklore question. If dozens of unconnected cultures, spread across multiple continents, report similar creatures with consistent physical descriptions, and if those descriptions vary in ways that correlate with local ecology and available prey species, you have something else. You might still have a folklore question; a very interesting one about the structure of human imagination and the way cultures process the experience of wilderness. But you might also have a zoological question, or an anthropological one, or some combination that does not yet have a disciplinary home.

The comparative method is the tool that lets you find out which.

How Comparison Works

The logic of comparison is borrowed from multiple disciplines, and its power comes from the interplay between similarity and difference.

In comparative anatomy, biologists examine the same structure across different species to determine which features are shared due to common ancestry and which arose independently. The wing of a bat, the wing of a bird, and the wing of an insect all solve the same problem; flight, but they solve it through different evolutionary paths. Recognizing the difference between homology (shared ancestry) and analogy (independent solutions to similar problems) is one of the foundational skills of modern biology.

In comparative mythology, scholars like Joseph Campbell and, more rigorously, researchers in the tradition of comparative folklore, examine similar stories across cultures to determine which elements reflect shared human psychology and which are culturally specific. The "hero's journey" archetype appears in traditions worldwide, but the details vary with geography, ecology, and social structure.

In comparative linguistics, the presence of cognate words across languages reveals historical connections between populations that might otherwise seem unrelated.

In every case, the method is the same: place things side by side, note what is shared and what differs, and use the pattern to generate hypotheses about origin, mechanism, and relationship.

This series applies that method to cryptids. Each volume takes three creatures that share a family resemblance; broadly similar physical descriptions, comparable habitats, overlapping behavioral reports, and examines them through a structured sequence. First, each creature is presented on its own terms: its sighting history, its cultural context, its physical evidence, its ecological setting. Then the three are placed side by side and the similarities and differences are mapped.

What the Comparison Reveals

The comparative approach generates insights that are not available to single-case studies. Some of the most important include:

Ecological calibration. If three cultures independently report a large, hair-covered bipedal creature, and the reported size, diet, and behavior of the creature vary in ways that correlate with local climate and available food sources, this is significant. It means the reports are not simply copying each other or drawing from a shared mythological template. They are responsive to local conditions, which is exactly what we would expect from reports of a real animal and somewhat harder to explain as pure invention.

Cultural fingerprinting. Conversely, if three sets of reports share specific details that do not correlate with local ecology; if they attribute the same supernatural powers, the same emotional associations, the same narrative role, this points toward a cultural or psychological explanation. It suggests that the creature, whatever its biological status, is also functioning as a symbol, and the symbolic content can be separated from the zoological content.

Evidence quality assessment. Comparing the evidence base across three cases allows you to see which types of evidence are robust and which are fragile. If footprint evidence is strong in one region and weak in another, the difference may tell you something about soil conditions, investigator quality, or the creature itself. If witness testimony is consistent across all three regions despite differences in culture and language, that consistency has evidential weight.

The range of the possible. Perhaps most importantly, the comparative method forces you to consider explanations that a single case would not suggest. If you study only Bigfoot, you might conclude that the creature, if real, is a surviving population of *Gigantopithecus blacki*, the enormous Asian ape known from the fossil record. But when you place Bigfoot alongside the Yowie and the Mapinguari; creatures reported from continents with very different paleontological histories, the *Gigantopithecus* hypothesis either needs to expand dramatically or yield to a different framework entirely. The comparison does not answer the question, but it sharpens it.

The Shape of This Book

With that framework in place, here is how this volume proceeds.

The first three chapters after this introduction present each creature individually. Bigfoot comes first, not because the North American case is strongest, but because it is the most extensively documented and the most familiar to the likely readership. The Mapinguari follows, bringing with it the dense ecology and indigenous knowledge systems of the Amazon basin. The Yowie comes third, with the unique biogeographic context of Australia and a sighting history that stretches back tens of thousands of years into Aboriginal oral tradition.

Once all three creatures are on the table, the book shifts to comparative analysis. Shared characteristics are mapped and examined. Differences are cataloged and interrogated. The absence of definitive physical evidence; the single most important fact about all three creatures, is addressed directly and at length. Methods of investigation are assessed. The psychology of encounter is explored. The ecological feasibility of hidden populations is modeled.

The later chapters widen the lens further, examining the noise that surrounds the signal, the translation problems that plague cross-cultural evidence, the institutional barriers to serious research, the economic and social incentives that distort reporting, and the possibility of building a meaningful taxonomy of creatures that have not been confirmed to exist.

The book closes by returning to the question of what these three creatures, taken together, suggest about the larger phenomenon, and what the next comparison might reveal.

This is the first volume. The pattern will repeat, with different creatures and different questions, across the series. Each book is designed to stand alone, but together they build a cumulative picture that no single volume could provide.

The empty spaces on the map may not contain what we expect. They may contain something stranger, or something more mundane, or something that does not fit our existing categories at all. The only way to find out is to look carefully, compare honestly, and follow the evidence.

That is what we are here to do.

Bloodlines of the Wild

There are monsters in every culture.

Some slither. Some fly. Some rise from deep water or descend from distant stars. The human imagination, given enough time and enough darkness, produces an endless bestiary of things that do not exist.

And yet.

Across three continents separated by oceans, languages, and tens of thousands of years of isolation, three cultures developed the same creature.

Not a dragon.

Not a serpent.

Not a god.

An upright walker.

Large. Hair-covered. Watching from the tree line.

The premise of this series is simple: some legends are not isolated.

They are related.

This is not a catalog of random cryptids. It is an examination of families.

The working hypothesis of **Cryptid Cousins** is that certain legendary beings share morphological, behavioral, and psychological continuity across geography. If they are biological, they may be divergent branches of a common ancestral line. If they are archetypal, they may emerge from a shared cognitive architecture embedded deeply in the human species.

In either case, the similarities are not accidental.

In this first volume, we examine three giants of wilderness testimony:

- Bigfoot of North America
- The Mapinguari of the Amazon Basin
- The Yowie of Australia

Different climates.

Different cultural lenses.

Different behavioral reputations.

And yet, the silhouette remains the same.

Each inhabits the edge.

Each carries the smell of animal musk and the weight of something older than settlement.

Each generates encounters defined not by predation, but by warning.

This book does not argue that these creatures are real.

It does not argue that they are imaginary.

It argues something more precise: that the phenomenon itself; the pattern, is worthy of serious, structured comparison.

To dismiss these reports outright is intellectually lazy.

To accept them uncritically is equally irresponsible.

Between those extremes lies a space for investigation.

Here, we examine testimony alongside paleontology.

Behavioral accounts alongside archetypal psychology.

Ecological adaptation alongside cultural interpretation.

We ask whether these beings represent:

- Surviving relict hominoids
- Cultural memory of extinct megafauna
- Deeply embedded archetypes of the Wild Man
- Or some convergence of all three

The goal is not resolution.

The goal is clarity.

If something moves at the edge of the firelight on three continents and leaves the same shape behind, the question is not whether the shape is comfortable.

The question is why it is consistent.

Welcome to Volume I.

The Great Hairy Humanoids.

The bloodline begins here.

Chapter 1: Bigfoot — The North American King

The Shadow in the Pines

Long before the word "Bigfoot" entered the American lexicon, the forests of the Pacific Northwest held a name for the thing that moved between the trees. The Sts'ailes people of British Columbia spoke of the Sasquatch; a word derived from their Halkomelem language, with a gravity that had nothing to do with campfire entertainment. To them, and to dozens of other indigenous nations stretching from the coastal rainforests of Washington to the boreal wilderness of northern Canada, the creature was not a legend. It was a neighbor.

The indigenous oral traditions surrounding the Sasquatch are remarkably consistent across nations that had little or no contact with one another. The Lummi spoke of the Ts'emekwes, a towering forest dweller that could be heard calling across the valleys at dusk. The Yakama warned of beings that inhabited the high ridges and could not be followed. The Coast Salish traditions describe a creature of immense size and strength that existed in a kind of parallel world; not entirely animal, not entirely spirit, but something that occupied a space the Western mind has always struggled to categorize. These were not fairy tales told to frighten children. They were practical warnings woven into the fabric of daily life, spoken with the same matter-of-fact tone one might use to describe the habits of a bear or the migration of elk.

It is worth pausing on this point, because it speaks to something that modern investigation has too often overlooked. For thousands of years, across hundreds of distinct cultures, the people who knew the North American wilderness most intimately, who lived within it, hunted within it, and built entire cosmologies around its rhythms, agreed that something large and bipedal shared the land with them. This was not a singular myth that spread from one tribe to the next like a game of telephone. It was a convergence of independent observation, and it deserves to be treated as such.

The modern chapter of the Bigfoot story, however, begins not with reverence but with a road.

In August of 1958, a bulldozer operator named Jerry Crew was working on a logging road near Bluff Creek in Humboldt County, California. The work was remote and grueling, pushing heavy equipment through dense old-growth forest in a region so isolated that supply runs were measured in days rather than hours. Crew arrived at his machine one morning to find something that stopped him cold: a series of enormous, humanlike footprints pressed deeply into the mud around his bulldozer. They were roughly sixteen inches long and sank into the earth with a weight that no human foot could have produced. Crew was not a man given to flights of fancy. He was a logger, a practical man who worked with his hands in one of the most unforgiving industries in North America. He made a plaster cast of one of the prints and carried it into the offices of the Humboldt Times. The newspaper ran the story, and the editor, Andrew Genzoli, used a term that would reshape an entire field of inquiry. He called the unknown trackmaker "Bigfoot."

The name stuck with the tenacity of a brand, and it spread through regional papers and eventually into the national consciousness. But the Bluff Creek incident was more than a naming event. It was a threshold. Before Crew brought his plaster cast out of the woods, the creature of indigenous tradition existed in a space that Western science and media could comfortably ignore. After Bluff Creek, it could not. The plaster cast was physical. It was measurable. It demanded, if not belief, then at least a response.

What followed was a slow-building wave of interest that would transform the Sasquatch from a regional curiosity into a fixture of American culture. Investigators and enthusiasts began combing the Pacific Northwest, interviewing loggers, hunters, and rural residents who had, in many cases, been sitting quietly on their own encounters for years. The accounts that emerged were strikingly uniform: a massive, upright figure covered in dark hair, moving through the forest with a silence that seemed impossible for something of its size. The witnesses were, more often than not, people who had spent their lives in the woods and had no interest in public attention. Many of them reported their encounters with visible reluctance, aware that speaking openly would invite ridicule.

Beyond the Tree Line: The Continental Footprint

The popular imagination places Bigfoot in the Pacific Northwest, and with good reason; the region's dense old-growth forests, massive tracts of unbroken wilderness, and deep cultural history of sightings have made it the epicenter of investigation for decades. But to treat Bigfoot as a Pacific Northwest phenomenon is to ignore the map.

The Bigfoot Field Researchers Organization, which maintains the most comprehensive public database of sighting reports in North America, has cataloged encounters from every state in the continental United States and every province of Canada. Reports are not distributed evenly; the Pacific Northwest, the Ohio River Valley, the Appalachian corridor from Pennsylvania through the Carolinas, the Gulf Coast states, and the forested regions of eastern Texas and Oklahoma generate the heaviest concentrations. But even states that seem inhospitable to the idea of a hidden primate: Illinois, New Jersey, Florida, contribute a steady, low-frequency stream of reports year after year.

This geographic spread poses both an opportunity and a problem for researchers. The opportunity is statistical: a phenomenon reported across such a vast range and such varied terrain, by thousands of independent witnesses, is harder to attribute to a single cultural narrative or a single tradition of hoaxing. The problem is ecological: a species with this kind of continental distribution would require either an enormous population or an extraordinary capacity for dispersal across fragmented habitats; a question the ecological feasibility chapters of this book will examine in detail.

What the geographic data does suggest, even to a cautious eye, is that if something is being seen, it is not confined to one forest or one mountain range. It is using the full depth of the North American wilderness, from the coastal rainforests of British Columbia to the swamp bottoms of the Deep South, and it has been doing so for as long as records of any kind have been kept.

The Question of Hoaxes

The Bluff Creek legacy is complicated. It is now widely acknowledged that some of the tracks found in the area during that period were likely hoaxed by Ray Wallace, a contractor with a well-documented love of practical jokes. Wallace's family revealed after his death in 2002 that he had possessed carved wooden feet, and they claimed he was responsible for the original prints. This revelation was seized upon by skeptics as a definitive debunking.

But the reality is more nuanced. The tracks that Crew cast, and others documented in the area by researchers such as Bob Titmus and John Green, display characteristics that do not align with simple wooden stompers; including variations in toe splay and depth distribution that suggest a flexible, living foot. Whether Wallace hoaxed some tracks does not automatically invalidate all tracks, and the tendency to conflate the two has been one of the more persistent errors in the public conversation around this subject.

What Bluff Creek ultimately gave the world was a starting point. It pulled the Sasquatch out of the realm of indigenous oral tradition and into the harsh light of modern scrutiny, where it would be debated, dismissed, investigated, and obsessed over for decades to come. The shadow in the pines had been given a name, and once named, it refused to disappear.

The Anatomy of a Titan

To speak of Bigfoot in physical terms is to enter a body of testimony that is, in its consistency, genuinely difficult to dismiss outright.

Country Cousins: Bigfoot, Mapinguari and the Yowie

Thousands of eyewitness accounts have been gathered over the past several decades from across the North American continent, and while individual reports vary in their details, the composite picture they paint is remarkably stable.

The creature is described as standing between seven and ten feet tall, with the majority of accounts placing it in the eight-to-nine-foot range. It walks upright on two legs with a gait that witnesses frequently describe as fluid and purposeful; not the awkward, shuffling movement one might expect from something bipedal and massive, but a smooth, ground-covering stride. The body is covered in hair, most commonly described as dark brown or black, though reddish-brown and even grey variants have been reported. The shoulders are enormously broad, often described as being wider than any human's by a significant margin, and the arms hang longer in proportion to the body than those of a typical person, reaching to or past the knees.

The face, where visible, is described as flat and wide, with a heavy brow ridge, deep-set eyes, and a nose that is broad and somewhat flattened. The mouth is wide. The expression, according to those who have been close enough to see it, is typically one of calm observation or, less frequently, open hostility. The neck is either very short or entirely absent, with the head appearing to sit directly on the shoulders; a feature that has led some researchers to speculate about a sagittal crest, the bony ridge found on the skulls of great apes that serves as an anchor point for massive jaw muscles.

This brings us to one of the more discussed anatomical features: the so-called "conical" skull shape. Multiple witnesses and several of the more detailed track and body proportion analyses have suggested that the Bigfoot cranium rises to a modest peak or cone at the top, rather than presenting the rounded dome of the human skull. This is consistent with a sagittal crest and would imply a creature with jaw strength far exceeding that of a human being. In the great apes, particularly adult male gorillas, the sagittal crest is a standard feature, and its potential presence in an unknown hominid would place the creature firmly within the framework of primate anatomy rather than outside it.

The Stench in the Record

There is one feature of the Bigfoot encounter that almost never appears in the dramatized versions, the television specials, or the casual retellings; and it is, paradoxically, one of the most consistently reported details in the firsthand accounts. The smell.

Witnesses describe it with the kind of visceral specificity that is difficult to invent: a thick, gagging stench variously compared to rotting meat, wet dog, sulfur, an open sewer, or the musk of a large animal amplified to an almost unbearable intensity. It does not merely accompany the sighting. In many reports, it precedes it; rolling through the trees like an invisible announcement, triggering nausea and a deep, instinctive alarm before the creature itself is ever seen.

The frequency and consistency of this detail across independent reports is striking. Witnesses in the temperate rainforests of Washington describe the same quality of odor as witnesses in the hardwood hollows of eastern Ohio or the cypress swamps of Florida. The language varies, but the experience is remarkably stable: an overwhelming biological stench, unlike any known wildlife in the area, strong enough to be detected from dozens of yards away and, in some cases, lingering at a site long after the encounter has ended.

From a biological standpoint, extreme body odor is neither unusual nor implausible in a large primate. The great apes are, as a group, notably pungent. Adult male gorillas produce a sharp, acrid scent from apocrine glands during periods of stress or social signaling; a smell strong enough to be detected by researchers at considerable distance. Orangutans produce distinctive musky odors that intensify with emotional arousal. In the broader animal kingdom, powerful scent is a standard tool of territorial marking, social communication, and predator deterrence.

If Bigfoot exists as a biological organism, a strong and distinctive body odor would be expected rather than surprising. What makes the smell significant as evidence is not its plausibility; it is its independence. The detail appears in reports from witnesses who have no knowledge of other reports, no familiarity with the research literature, and no reason to fabricate a detail that adds nothing to the drama of the story but everything to its biological consistency. It is the kind of detail that a storyteller would leave out and a real encounter would leave in.

The Evidence Underfoot

But it is the footprints that have provided the most tangible and scientifically analyzable evidence. Thousands of prints have been cast, photographed, and measured over the years, and while many are undoubtedly hoaxes; the product of carved feet and deliberate deception, a significant number display features that are extraordinarily difficult to fabricate.

The most discussed of these features is the mid-tarsal break. In human feet, the tarsal bones of the midfoot are locked into a rigid arch that acts as a lever during walking. This arch is one of the defining adaptations of human bipedalism. In the footprints attributed to Bigfoot, however, the midfoot appears to flex in a way that suggests a fundamentally different skeletal structure; one where the tarsal joint bends during the stride, producing a pressure ridge across the middle of the print. Dr. Jeff Meldrum, a professor of anatomy and anthropology at Idaho State University, has been one of the most prominent scientific voices on this subject. His analysis of numerous track casts has led him to conclude that the mid-tarsal break is consistent with a foot adapted for bipedal locomotion on uneven, forested terrain; a foot that sacrifices the spring-loaded efficiency of the human arch for greater flexibility and grip.

The implications of this are significant. If the mid-tarsal break is genuine; and Meldrum's work suggests that at least some of the casts exhibiting it are not the product of hoaxing, then the creature responsible for the prints possesses a foot that is neither human nor ape, but something in between. It is a foot built for a different kind of walking, one suited to the soft, uneven ground of deep forest rather than the open savannah that shaped the human gait.

Beyond the mid-tarsal break, the prints themselves reveal details that speak to a living, biological foot. Dermal ridges: the equivalent of fingerprints, have been identified on several casts, most notably those examined by forensic analyst Jimmy Chilcutt, who spent his career analyzing primate fingerprints for law enforcement. Chilcutt reported that the ridge patterns he observed on certain Bigfoot casts were distinct from those of humans and known apes, displaying a flow pattern unlike anything in his reference database. Whether this constitutes proof is a matter of ongoing debate, but it represents the kind of physical detail that is extremely difficult to engineer into a hoax.

Beyond Footprints

The footprint record is the most extensive body of physical evidence associated with Bigfoot, but it is not the only one.

In September of 2000, a team of researchers from the Bigfoot Field Researchers Organization conducted an expedition in the Gifford Pinchot National Forest in Washington State. They placed fruit bait near a muddy wallow; a depression in the ground where elk and other wildlife come to roll in wet earth. When they returned the following morning, they found what appeared to be a large body impression in the mud. The impression, which was carefully cast in plaster over the course of several hours, showed what researchers identified as the imprint of a large forearm, a massive thigh, a heel, and what appeared to be an Achilles tendon; all at proportions significantly larger than any human could produce.

The Skookum Cast, as it became known, was examined by Dr. Jeff Meldrum, Dr. Grover Krantz, and Dr. John Bindernagel, among others.

Their assessments varied in confidence but converged on a key point: the impression did not match the anatomy of any known North American wildlife, including elk, bear, or human. The hair samples recovered from the cast were analyzed and found to be primate in character but not identifiable to a known species. Skeptics have argued that the impression was made by an elk lying in the mud, and this explanation cannot be entirely ruled out. But the anatomical details visible in the cast; particularly the apparent Achilles tendon impression and the proportions of the forearm, are difficult to reconcile with cervid anatomy.

Hair samples attributed to Bigfoot have been collected from sighting locations for decades, and their analysis tells a frustratingly incomplete story. Many samples, when subjected to microscopic examination, turn out to belong to known species, bear, deer, human, dog. A smaller number have been classified by hair morphology experts as "primate, species unknown"; a designation that is intriguing but far from definitive, as hair analysis alone cannot identify a species with certainty.

The emergence of environmental DNA sampling; the extraction of genetic material from soil, water, and air, represents what may be the most promising frontier in physical evidence collection. Several research teams have begun deploying eDNA techniques in areas of reported Bigfoot activity, though published results to date have not produced confirmed unknown primate DNA. The method is still being refined for use in the specific habitats and conditions relevant to Bigfoot research, and its potential remains largely untapped.

The anatomy of Bigfoot, as assembled from the available evidence, does not describe a monster or a myth. It describes an animal; a large, bipedal primate adapted to a specific ecological niche. Whether that animal exists in the flesh or only in the accumulated weight of human testimony is the question that remains unanswered. But the physical profile, taken on its own terms, is internally consistent and biologically plausible in ways that deserve more serious attention than they have traditionally received.

The Men Who Staked Their Names

The scientific study of Bigfoot, such as it is, has been carried forward not by institutions but by individuals, and the cost of that work has, in most cases, been borne personally.

Grover Krantz was a physical anthropologist at Washington State University who, in the early 1970s, became the first tenured professor at a major research institution to publicly endorse the likelihood that Bigfoot was a real, biological species. Krantz examined track casts, analyzed reported anatomical proportions, and ultimately concluded that the evidence pointed toward a surviving population of *Gigantopithecus blacki*, the enormous Asian ape known from fossil teeth and jawbones found in China and Southeast Asia. His willingness to say so openly; in papers, in lectures, and on the record, effectively ended his chances of academic advancement. He was denied promotions, marginalized within his department, and treated, by his own account, as a cautionary tale for junior colleagues who might be tempted to pursue similar interests. He continued the work until his death in 2002, donating his skeleton to the Smithsonian Institution; where, in a final irony, it was displayed alongside the bones of the creatures he had spent his career studying.

John Green, a Canadian journalist and investigator, spent more than four decades collecting and cataloging Bigfoot sighting reports across North America. His database, painstakingly assembled from newspaper accounts, personal interviews, and field investigations, remains one of the most comprehensive records of the phenomenon ever compiled. Green approached the subject with the methodical skepticism of a working journalist: he verified sources, cross-referenced accounts, and discarded reports that did not meet his standards of credibility. His published works, including *Sasquatch:*

The Apes Among Us, are models of careful documentation and remain essential references.

René Dahinden, a Swiss-Canadian researcher, devoted virtually his entire adult life to the pursuit of physical evidence for Bigfoot. Dahinden's approach was relentlessly field-oriented; he spent years in the forests of British Columbia, following up on sighting reports, casting tracks, and interviewing witnesses. He was also a fierce advocate for evidentiary standards within the research community, frequently clashing with investigators whose methods he considered sloppy or whose conclusions he found premature. Dahinden's life is a study in the personal cost of pursuing an answer that never quite arrives: he spent his savings, strained his relationships, and died in 2001 without the definitive proof he had spent decades seeking.

These men: and they are representative of a broader community of serious investigators, including Peter Byrne, Thomas Steenburg, and others, are important not because they proved Bigfoot exists but because they demonstrated what disciplined investigation of the subject looks like. Their work established methodological baselines for track analysis, witness interviewing, and evidence preservation that the field continues to rely on. And their personal sacrifices illustrate a truth that the later chapters of this book will examine in detail: the institutional barriers to cryptid research are not merely intellectual. They are social, professional, and deeply personal.

The Patterson Legacy

On October 20, 1967, two men on horseback rode into a remote stretch of Bluff Creek, California, and emerged with what would become the single most scrutinized piece of evidence in the history of cryptozoology. Roger Patterson and Bob Gimlin were not scientists. Patterson was a rodeo rider and aspiring filmmaker with a deep personal interest in the Bigfoot phenomenon. Gimlin was a rancher and experienced outdoorsman who had agreed to accompany his friend on what was, by most measures, a speculative expedition into the wilderness. What happened in the creek bed that afternoon would define both their lives.

The film, shot on a rented 16mm Kodak camera, runs for just under a minute. It shows a large, dark, hair-covered figure walking upright along the sandbar of the creek. The creature turns to look back at the camera; a moment that has been frozen, enlarged, enhanced, and debated for over half a century, and then continues walking with a deliberate, unhurried stride into the tree line and out of frame. The figure is clearly female; prominent breasts are visible. The gait is smooth and powerful. The muscles of the thighs and back appear to flex and shift beneath the hair in a way that suggests a living body in motion.

The Patterson-Gimlin film has been analyzed by everyone from Hollywood special effects artists to biomechanics researchers, and the conclusions are anything but unanimous. Skeptics have argued that the figure is a man in a suit, and over the years, several individuals have claimed: or been claimed by others, to be the person inside it. None of these claims have been substantiated with physical evidence, and many are mutually contradictory. The most frequently cited, involving a man named Bob Heironimus, relies entirely on his personal testimony and has been disputed by multiple researchers who have examined the film in detail.

On the other side, serious analysis has raised points that are difficult to reconcile with the suit hypothesis. The proportions of the figure; particularly the arm length relative to the torso and the breadth of the shoulders, do not match human anatomy. The apparent muscle movement beneath the surface of the body is inconsistent with any known costume technology available in 1967. Bill Munns, a professional creature and makeup effects artist with decades of experience in Hollywood, conducted an exhaustive, multi-year analysis of the film and concluded that fabricating the figure with the materials and techniques available at the time would have been extraordinarily difficult, if not impossible. Munns' analysis addressed everything from the hair pattern to the limb proportions to the way light fell across the body, and his findings have never been effectively rebutted.

The film occupies a unique and uncomfortable space in the Bigfoot discourse. It is too compelling to ignore and too controversial to accept. It has been called the greatest piece of evidence for an unknown primate and the most elaborate hoax in the history of wildlife documentation, and reasonable people have landed on both sides. What is not in dispute is its impact. The Patterson-Gimlin film transformed Bigfoot from a regional curiosity into a global phenomenon and set the terms for every investigation that followed.

The Biomechanics of the Bluff Creek Figure

Beyond questions of motive and costume capability lies a quieter and more technical issue: locomotion.

Human beings are remarkably consistent walkers. Even trained actors inside prosthetic suits struggle to alter the fundamental rhythm of bipedal motion. The center of gravity, the hip sway, the arm swing arc; these are neurologically patterned and exceedingly difficult to disguise without extensive training.

Frame-by-frame stabilization of the Patterson-Gimlin film has allowed researchers to analyze stride length, knee lift, and arm extension. The figure's stride measures approximately 41 inches at its widest interval, notably longer than the average stride length of a six-foot human male walking at comparable speed. More striking than the stride length is the flexion pattern of the knee and ankle joints. The figure does not display the stiff-kneed "costume walk" typical of hoaxed footage. Instead, there is visible compliance in the knee joint during weight transfer and a smooth mid-stance phase consistent with trained bipedal locomotion.

The arm swing ratio has received particular attention. In humans, relaxed gait produces arm motion that rarely exceeds the upper thigh. The Bluff Creek figure's arms swing downward well past the mid-thigh, approaching the knee. When adjusted for estimated height, this suggests humeral proportions outside standard human anatomical ratios. A human wearing arm extensions would be required to significantly alter scapular and shoulder rotation to replicate this fluidity; something even modern film productions struggle to achieve convincingly.

The most debated element remains muscle movement. High-resolution digitizations have revealed apparent muscle flexion along the quadriceps and gastrocnemius regions during stride. Skeptics argue that this could represent fabric shifting. However, the movement appears localized and structurally consistent with subcutaneous muscle groups, not loose surface material. In 1967, flexible foam latex muscle suits of this complexity were not commercially available, and no documented production facility of the era possessed the budget or craftsmanship required to manufacture one in secrecy.

Center-of-mass analysis offers another complication. The figure appears slightly forward-leaning but balanced; a posture consistent with a body carrying significant upper torso mass. Humans attempting to simulate this while wearing weight-distributing prosthetics would exhibit compensatory movement in the hips. The Patterson figure does not.

None of these points individually prove authenticity. But collectively, they raise the evidentiary bar for the "man in a suit" explanation far higher than casual dismissal suggests.

The Voice in the Dark

But the visual evidence is only one dimension of the Bigfoot encounter. There is also the auditory dimension, and it is here that the investigation takes on a different, more visceral character.

Throughout the late twentieth century, researchers working in remote wilderness areas began recording sounds that did not match any known wildlife. These vocalizations, captured on audio equipment left running overnight in areas with reported activity, include a range of sounds: howls, whoops, grunts, and a sustained, resonating scream that has become known in the research community as the "Primal Scream." The recordings vary in quality, but the best of them; particularly those captured in the Sierra Nevada range and in the forests of the Pacific Northwest, have been subjected to spectrographic analysis and found to possess characteristics that are, by the assessment of the audio experts who have examined them, difficult to attribute to any catalogued animal.

The frequency range, the volume as estimated from distance calculations, and the tonal complexity of these vocalizations suggest a chest cavity and vocal apparatus of considerable size. Some researchers have drawn comparisons to the long-distance calls of great apes, particularly the howling of gibbons and the chest-beat vocalizations of gorillas, noting that the recorded sounds share certain structural features with primate communication while remaining distinct from any known species.

The psychological impact of these sounds on those who have heard them firsthand should not be underestimated. Witnesses consistently describe a deep, involuntary fear response; a gut-level reaction that goes beyond surprise or confusion. Experienced outdoorsmen, people who have spent decades in bear and cougar country without flinching, have described being reduced to a state of near-paralysis by the sound. There is something in the quality of the vocalization that seems to bypass rational thought and speak directly to an older, more primal part of the human brain. Whether this is evidence of a biological creature or simply the power of the unknown to unsettle the human psyche is, once again, a matter of interpretation. But the consistency of the response across independent witnesses, separated by thousands of miles and decades of time, is a data point that resists easy dismissal.

The Sierra Sounds

Among the recorded vocalizations attributed to Bigfoot, none have generated more analysis or more controversy than the Sierra Sounds; a series of recordings made by Al Berry and Ron Morehead in the Sierra Nevada mountains of California between 1971 and 1974.

Berry and Morehead were experienced outdoorsmen who had been drawn to a remote hunting camp at an elevation of approximately 8,000 feet by reports of unusual activity in the area. Over multiple visits spanning several years, they captured hours of audio using reel-to-reel recording equipment left running overnight. The recordings include a range of vocalizations; deep guttural sounds, high-pitched chattering, sustained howls, but the most remarkable segments contain what sounds unmistakably like rapid, articulate speech in a language no one has been able to identify.

The recordings were analyzed by R. Scott Nelson, a retired U.S. Navy cryptolinguist who had spent his career studying the structure of human language for military intelligence purposes. Nelson concluded that the vocalizations exhibited features consistent with structured language: identifiable phonemes, repeated morphological units, apparent syntax, and variation that suggested semantic content rather than random vocalization. He published a partial phonetic transcription of the recordings and stated publicly that, in his professional assessment, what the tapes captured was not animal vocalization but language; produced by a species whose vocal apparatus differed from a human's but whose communication met the functional criteria of linguistic structure.

Nelson's analysis has not been replicated by other linguists, and the recordings remain controversial. Skeptics have proposed that the sounds were produced by humans; either as a deliberate hoax or as misidentified activity from other camps in the area. Supporters note that the recordings were made at a remote location, at high altitude, over multiple years, and that the vocal characteristics; particularly the speed, frequency range, and simultaneous multi-tonal production, are difficult to reproduce with the human vocal tract.

The Sierra Sounds do not prove the existence of Bigfoot. But if the linguistic analysis is even partially correct, they suggest something more unsettling than a large animal in the woods. They suggest a large animal that talks.

The Nightfall Question

There is a pattern buried in the sighting data that any serious investigation must confront: the majority of close-range Bigfoot encounters occur between dusk and dawn.

This is not merely a function of human activity patterns or reduced visibility. Witnesses camping, hunting, or traveling at night report a suite of features that suggest the creature is specifically adapted to low-light conditions. The most frequently cited is eye shine; a reflective glow from the eyes when struck by flashlight, headlamp, or vehicle headlights. The reported color is most often reddish-orange or amber, though yellow and green have also been described. Eye shine in mammals is produced by the tapetum lucidum, a reflective layer behind the retina that amplifies available light, and is found in a wide range of nocturnal and crepuscular species. It is not present in humans or in any of the known great apes.

If reliable, the presence of a tapetum lucidum in Bigfoot would be a significant anatomical distinction; one that separates it from the ape lineage most commonly proposed as its closest relative and suggests adaptation to a niche where low-light activity is a primary survival strategy. It would also help explain the persistent elusiveness of the creature: an animal that conducts the majority of its activity during the hours when human observers are least present and least visually capable would be, almost by definition, extraordinarily difficult to document.

The nocturnal pattern also has implications for the photographic evidence, or rather the lack of it. The question "Why hasn't anyone gotten a clear photograph?" is among the most common objections raised against the existence of Bigfoot. The answer, if the nocturnal data is taken seriously, is straightforward: because clear photographs are extraordinarily difficult to obtain of any large animal that is primarily active in darkness, avoids human contact, and operates in dense forest cover. Camera traps, which have been deployed in numerous Bigfoot research areas, are optimized for animals that use established game trails. A creature intelligent enough to avoid trails, active primarily at night, and inhabiting terrain with dense canopy cover would be precisely the kind of animal that camera traps are least effective at capturing.

This does not resolve the photographic problem. It contextualizes it.

Case Study: The Siege at Ape Canyon (1924)

In the summer of 1924, a small group of prospectors working near the slopes of Mount St. Helens reported what remains one of the most dramatic encounters in Bigfoot history. The men: Fred Beck, Marion Smith, and several companions, had established a crude cabin in a remote ravine later known as Ape Canyon. The terrain was steep, heavily forested, and largely inaccessible except by foot or pack animal.

According to Beck's later published account, the incident began when the men observed a large, upright figure at a distance near their mining site. Beck claimed he fired his rifle at the figure, believing it posed a threat. The creature fell, then regained its footing and disappeared into the forest. That evening, events escalated.

Shortly after dark, the men reported hearing heavy footfalls outside their cabin. What followed was described as a coordinated assault. Large rocks: some reportedly weighing several pounds, were thrown against the cabin walls and roof throughout the night. The men, armed and barricaded inside, stated that the bombardment continued for hours. They claimed to hear multiple entities circling the structure, communicating with one another through grunts and guttural sounds. At dawn, the activity ceased.

When the miners descended from the cabin, they reported finding large footprints in the vicinity, though no verifiable casts were preserved. Newspapers of the time referred to the attackers as "mountain devils," a label reflecting both fear and uncertainty rather than zoological clarity.

Skeptics have long argued that the siege narrative was embellished or fabricated for attention. Others note that the isolated geography, the consistency of multiple witness testimony, and the reported rock-throwing behavior align with recurring modern Bigfoot encounter patterns. Rock throwing, in particular, has since become a commonly reported territorial behavior in North American Bigfoot cases.

The Ape Canyon incident occupies a peculiar space in the record. It is too dramatic to accept casually and too consistent with later reports to dismiss outright. Whether it reflects a genuine encounter with unknown primates or a collision of isolation, fear, and narrative escalation remains unresolved. What it demonstrates unmistakably is that the Bigfoot phenomenon was already well-formed in its behavioral patterning long before the Patterson film brought it into global awareness.

The Behavioral Catalog

The Ape Canyon siege introduced a behavior; the hurling of rocks, that has since become one of the most frequently reported elements of Bigfoot encounters. But it is only one entry in a behavioral catalog that, taken as a whole, suggests a creature of considerable cognitive complexity.

Wood knocking is perhaps the most commonly reported auditory behavior after vocalizations. Witnesses and field researchers describe hearing loud, resonant strikes; as if a heavy branch or log were being slammed against a tree trunk, echoing through the forest, often in apparent sequences. In some cases, researchers have reported call-and-response patterns: a knock delivered from one ridge answered by a knock from another, separated by distances that rule out a single source. The sound is distinct from the drumming of woodpeckers, the cracking of deadfall, or the territorial tree-slapping of bears. It is deliberate, rhythmic, and, in the accounts of those who have heard it, unmistakably intentional.

Tree structures represent a more controversial category of evidence. In areas with reported Bigfoot activity, investigators have documented formations of bent and woven saplings; young trees twisted at heights of six to ten feet and interlocked with neighboring trunks to form arches, X-shapes, or crude lean-to configurations. Similar formations have been reported across widely separated regions with no apparent natural explanation. Wind damage, snow loading, and the territorial marking behavior of bears and elk have all been proposed and, in individual cases, may account for specific structures. But the consistency of the formations; their height, their apparent intentionality, their concentration in active sighting areas, has led some researchers to propose them as territorial markers or shelter-building behavior.

Paralleling describes a behavior reported by hikers, hunters, and campers in which a large, unseen or partially seen figure moves through the forest on a course parallel to their own, maintaining a consistent distance and matching their pace. The behavior is typically detected through sound; heavy footfalls in the undergrowth, the snapping of branches at regular intervals, and occasionally confirmed by brief visual contact. Witnesses describe the experience as deeply unnerving, not because of any overt threat but because of the obvious intelligence it implies. The creature is not fleeing. It is not approaching. It is observing, and it is doing so with a degree of spatial awareness and intentional movement that suggests something well beyond the behavioral range of any known North American wildlife.

Bluff charging and intimidation displays appear in a smaller but consistent subset of reports. These typically involve a sudden, explosive approach; crashing through brush, vocalizing loudly, that stops short of actual physical contact. The behavior mirrors intimidation displays documented in gorillas, chimpanzees, and other great apes, where the goal is to establish dominance or drive away a perceived threat without engaging in a physical confrontation that could result in injury.

Taken individually, each of these behaviors admits alternative explanation. Taken together and observed across independent reports from witnesses who had no knowledge of the broader behavioral pattern, they describe something that behaves less like a simple animal and more like an intelligent, socially organized primate, one that communicates over distance, modifies its environment, monitors intruders, and employs graduated threat responses. This behavioral profile does not prove the existence of the creature. But it significantly narrows the range of plausible explanations for the reports themselves.

What the Forest Provides

The question of what Bigfoot eats has received less attention than questions of anatomy or behavior, but it is no less important; particularly for the ecological modeling that later chapters of this book will undertake.

The available evidence, drawn from witness reports, site investigations, and the analysis of scat samples of uncertain provenance, suggests an omnivorous diet broadly consistent with that of other large-bodied primates. Witnesses have reported observing the creatures foraging for roots, tubers, and berries. In the Pacific Northwest, the seasonal availability of salmonberries, huckleberries, and skunk cabbage roots has led some researchers to propose a diet anchored in high-calorie plant material supplemented by opportunistic protein sources; a pattern that closely mirrors the dietary strategy of black bears sharing the same habitat.

The protein component is more contentious. A subset of reports describe predation on deer, with witnesses claiming to have observed or found evidence of large ungulates killed and partially consumed in ways inconsistent with known predator behavior in the area. Livestock predation: particularly of pigs and goats in rural areas adjacent to forest, appears occasionally in the report literature, though it is nearly impossible to distinguish from predation by bears, cougars, or feral dogs without direct observation.

Fish represent another proposed food source, particularly in the Pacific Northwest during salmon spawning runs, when enormous concentrations of protein are available in shallow waterways. Several researchers have noted that peak Bigfoot sighting activity in certain river systems correlates with spawning season; a pattern that, if genuine, would link the creature's movement to an established ecological event and provide a framework for predictive research.

The dietary question matters because it connects directly to population viability. A large-bodied omnivore in temperate or subtropical forest requires a substantial home range and a reliable caloric baseline. Estimating those requirements and comparing them against the carrying capacity of the habitats where sightings concentrate, is one of the more productive lines of inquiry available to researchers working within the constraints of unconfirmed evidence.

The Persistence of the Shadow

The legacy of Bigfoot; from the oral traditions of indigenous nations to the plaster casts of Bluff Creek, from the Patterson film to the Sierra Sounds, from the behavioral patterns reported by solitary hunters to the institutional sacrifices of Grover Krantz, is not one of proof. It is one of persistence.

The evidence is incomplete, contested, and frustratingly ambiguous. But it has not gone away. Each decade has added new accounts, new analysis, and new technology brought to bear on the old questions. The sighting reports continue to accumulate; not from a single region or a single demographic, but from across an entire continent, from people with nothing to gain and credibility to lose. The physical evidence remains suggestive without being conclusive. The behavioral patterns repeat with a consistency that demands explanation, even if that explanation falls short of a confirmed species.

And the shadow in the pines; whatever it may be, continues to move just beyond the reach of certainty.

In the chapters that follow, we will place this creature beside two others: the Mapinguari of the Amazon and the Yowie of Australia. They share with Bigfoot a broad physical description, a deep indigenous history, and the same maddening position on the evidence spectrum; too present to ignore, too elusive to confirm. What the comparison reveals about all three, and about the phenomenon they represent, is the work that lies ahead.

Chapter 2: Mapinguari — The Amazonian Beast

The Roar of the Rainforest

The Amazon Basin is the largest tropical rainforest on Earth; a vast, breathing organism of roughly two million square miles that sprawls across nine nations and contains, by even conservative estimates, more undiscovered species than any other ecosystem on the planet. It is a place where the canopy closes so completely that the forest floor exists in a state of perpetual twilight, where rivers run black with tannins and entire indigenous communities live their lives without meaningful contact with the outside world. If any landscape on Earth could conceal a large, unknown creature, it is this one.

But the Amazon is not a single, undifferentiated wilderness. It is a mosaic; a patchwork of *terra firme* forests that never flood, *várzea* floodplains that are submerged for months each year, *igapó* blackwater swamps, and vast stretches of transitional habitat where forest gives way to cerrado grassland and back again. These distinctions matter, because the creature at the center of this chapter is not reported uniformly across the basin. It is reported from specific kinds of places, and those places tell us something.

The Mapinguari; the name itself carries weight in a dozen languages across the basin, is most consistently associated with the deep *terra firme* forests of the western Brazilian Amazon, particularly in the states of Acre, Rondônia, and Amazonas, and along the tributaries of the Madeira and Purus river systems. These are among the most remote and least explored regions in the basin, places where the forest canopy stretches unbroken for hundreds of miles and where human presence, even indigenous human presence, thins to nearly nothing. It is in these deep interiors, far from the river highways that have served as the Amazon's primary corridors of travel and settlement for millennia, that the creature is spoken of most frequently, and most seriously.

Among the Karitiana, the Machiguenga, the Kaxinawá, and numerous other groups, the Mapinguari is not discussed lightly. It occupies a space in oral tradition that is less folklore and more cautionary geography. It is a marker of places not to go, a living boundary between the human world and the deeper, older forest that does not welcome visitors.

The accounts describe a creature of enormous size, bipedal or occasionally described as moving on all fours, that inhabits the most remote and inaccessible regions of the rainforest. But it is not the size that dominates the testimony. It is the smell.

The Stench That Arrives First

Virtually every account of the Mapinguari, whether collected by anthropologists, journalists, or field researchers, includes a description of a stench so overpowering that it causes nausea, disorientation, and in some accounts, temporary incapacitation. Witnesses have struggled to find adequate comparisons, settling most often on a combination of rotting flesh and feces of almost chemical intensity. Some accounts add a metallic quality to the odor, a sharpness underneath the organic decay that suggests something more complex than simple decomposition. This olfactory signature is so central to the Mapinguari experience that many indigenous accounts describe the smell arriving before the creature itself; rolling through the undergrowth like a wave, giving the forest a few moments of warning before the thing that produced it appears.

For a book that has already introduced the smell associated with Bigfoot encounters in North America, this convergence should register immediately. Two sets of cultures, separated by thousands of miles and entirely different ecological contexts, independently report that the most distinctive feature of their respective unknown creature is not its size, its appearance, or its behavior; it is an overwhelming biological stench. The details differ in ways that are worth noting: the Bigfoot odor is most often compared to wet animal musk and sulfur, while the

Mapinguari stench tends toward the putrid and fecal. But the underlying pattern; a smell so powerful that it precedes the creature, causes physiological distress, and is remembered more vividly than any visual detail, is remarkably consistent.

From a biological standpoint, the Mapinguari's odor admits several explanations. Large mammals commonly produce powerful scent through apocrine glands, anal scent glands, or specialized musk organs. In the context of the Amazon, where visibility in dense understory is often limited to a few dozen yards, chemical signaling would be an extraordinarily effective means of territorial communication; broadcasting presence and dominance over a wide area without requiring visual contact. A large, solitary, territorial animal in this environment would benefit enormously from the ability to announce itself chemically before any physical encounter occurs. The incapacitating quality described in some accounts is more difficult to explain through conventional biology, though not impossible. Some mammals, particularly mustelids like the wolverine and certain species of civet, produce secretions capable of causing nausea and disorientation at close range. Scaled up to the body mass implied by Mapinguari accounts, a similar glandular system could plausibly produce the effects described.

The smell, more than any other single feature, is what separates the Mapinguari accounts from casual myth-making. It is an unglamorous, unpleasant, physiologically specific detail that serves no narrative purpose. It does not make the creature more frightening in a storybook sense. It makes it more real.

The Voice That Carries

The vocalizations are equally distinctive. The Mapinguari is said to produce a roar or a sustained, bellowing cry that carries through the dense forest with startling clarity. Descriptions of this sound consistently emphasize two qualities: its volume and its effect on the listener. This is a deep, resonant call that produces a visceral fear response not unlike what has been reported by Bigfoot witnesses in North America; a sound that seems to bypass rational assessment and trigger something older, something written into the nervous system at a level that precedes language.

The cry is sometimes described as being preceded by the sound of heavy, rhythmic footfalls, as though the creature is announcing its approach with a deliberate, almost ritualistic cadence. Other accounts describe the vocalization as stationary; a sustained bellow delivered from a fixed position, as if the creature is staking a territorial claim rather than pursuing an intruder. The distinction matters, because it suggests different behavioral contexts for the sound: one associated with movement and active assertion, the other with boundary defense. In the acoustic environment of the Amazon, where the dense canopy absorbs high-frequency sounds and allows low-frequency calls to propagate over remarkable distances, a deep, resonant vocalization would be an optimal communication strategy for a large territorial animal. Howler monkeys, which produce the loudest calls of any land animal relative to their body size, exploit exactly this acoustic niche; their low-frequency roars can carry for miles through the forest. A creature several times the mass of a howler monkey, with a proportionally larger vocal apparatus, could theoretically produce a call audible across an entire river valley.

No confirmed recordings of the Mapinguari vocalization exist; a gap in the evidence that is frustrating but consistent with the extreme remoteness of the reported habitat. The acoustic monitoring technology that has been deployed in Bigfoot research areas in North America has not, to date, been systematically deployed in the deep Amazon. This represents one of the more promising avenues for future investigation, particularly given advances in autonomous recording units that can operate for months in tropical conditions without maintenance.

The Witnesses the World Overlooked

What makes the Mapinguari accounts particularly compelling from an investigative standpoint is their geographical breadth and temporal depth. These are not stories confined to a single village or a single generation. They have been collected from communities separated by hundreds of miles of impenetrable jungle, communities with no history of contact with one another, across a span of time that stretches back as far as oral tradition can reliably reach. The consistency of the core details; the size, the smell, the roar, the deep-forest habitat, across such a wide and disconnected sample is the kind of pattern that, in any other field of inquiry, would be taken seriously as evidence of a real phenomenon.

But there is a class of witness in the Mapinguari story that deserves particular attention, because they occupy a unique position in the history of Amazonian testimony: the *seringueiros*, the rubber tappers. During the rubber boom of the late nineteenth and early twentieth centuries, and continuing in diminished form through the latter decades of the twentieth century, tens of thousands of men were drawn into the deep Amazon to extract latex from wild rubber trees. The work was solitary by nature. A tapper would be assigned a circuit; a *Estrada*, of a hundred or more rubber trees spread across several miles of forest, and he would walk that circuit alone, day after day, spending the majority of his waking hours in some of the most remote and biologically dense forest on Earth. These men were not indigenous. Most were migrants from northeastern Brazil, *nordestinos* who came to the Amazon with no cultural framework for the Mapinguari and no prior exposure to indigenous oral traditions. They were practical laborers operating in extreme isolation.

And they came back with stories.

The rubber tapper testimony, collected by researchers including David Oren over the course of decades, is significant precisely because of what the tappers were not. They were not indigenous storytellers maintaining a cultural tradition. They were not explorers seeking adventure or fame. They were working men who had spent months alone in the forest and who reported encountering something that did not fit into their understanding of the natural world. The emotional register of their accounts is consistent: confusion, fear, and a reluctance to speak publicly that mirrors the pattern observed among rural Bigfoot witnesses in North America. Many tappers would only discuss their experiences after establishing trust with the interviewer, and several insisted on anonymity, aware that their accounts would be met with ridicule.

The details they provided; the smell, the sound, the size, the dense fur, the upright posture, aligned with the indigenous accounts they had never heard. This convergence between two entirely separate witness populations, one with deep cultural knowledge of the forest and one with none, is one of the strongest arguments against a purely cultural explanation for the Mapinguari phenomenon.

The Ancient Survivor

The physical description of the Mapinguari, as assembled from the body of available accounts, presents a creature that is both fascinating and deeply strange. It is described as standing roughly six to eight feet tall when upright, though some accounts place it larger. The body is covered in long, coarse, reddish-brown fur; a detail that is remarkably consistent across reports. The fur is often described as being so thick and matted that it appears almost armor-like, hanging from the body in heavy, tangled layers that give the creature a shaggy, almost prehistoric appearance.

The creature's movement is described in variable terms. Most accounts depict it as bipedal, walking upright with a heavy, deliberate gait. A smaller but consistent subset describe it as capable of quadrupedal locomotion as well, dropping to all fours when moving through dense undergrowth or when feeding. This dual-mode locomotion, if accurately reported, would be unusual but not unprecedented in the animal kingdom. Great apes are capable of both bipedal and quadrupedal movement, as were many extinct species of ground sloths, which could rear up on their hind legs to browse high vegetation while typically moving on all fours.

The arms are described as long and powerful, ending in hands that some accounts say bear large, curved claws; a detail that aligns with no known primate but aligns precisely with the anatomy of ground sloths, whose massive claws were among their most distinctive features. The face is described in fewer and less consistent terms than the body, likely owing to the fact that most encounters occur in conditions of poor visibility or at distances that do not permit detailed observation. Where facial features are described, witnesses mention a small head relative to the body, a flattened or forward-jutting face, and a wide mouth.

The Backward Feet

Two physical details set the Mapinguari apart from virtually every other reported cryptid on the planet. The first is its feet. Multiple accounts describe the creature as having feet that face backward; the toes pointing behind the creature rather than in front.

This detail has been a source of considerable discussion. On one level, it reads as pure mythology, the kind of disorienting, logic-defying detail that cultures worldwide have attached to supernatural beings as a way of signaling their otherness. The *Curupira*, another figure from Amazonian folklore, is also described with backward feet, as are forest spirits in traditions from West Africa, Southeast Asia, and the Philippines. The motif is nearly universal in tropical forest cultures, and its recurrence suggests a deep psychological function: backward feet invert the most basic navigational logic of tracking. They transform the forest from a readable landscape into an unreadable one. They say, in symbolic terms: *you cannot follow this thing. It does not move by your rules.*

On another level, the backward-feet motif may carry a kernel of observational truth. A creature with significantly different foot anatomy; one adapted to a very different mode of locomotion than the human norm, might produce tracks that appear to point in the opposite direction of travel. Ground sloths, whose feet were structured so that they walked on the outer edges and knuckles of their hind feet with the claws curled inward, left tracks that would have looked profoundly wrong to a human tracker accustomed to reading the prints of jaguars, tapirs, and peccaries. A large animal leaving unfamiliar, apparently reversed tracks in soft forest soil could easily generate exactly the kind of confusion that the backward-feet tradition describes.

Whether the detail is symbolic, observational, or some fusion of both, it is worth noting that it appears in Mapinguari accounts from communities that are separated by vast distances and have no evident mechanism for sharing this specific motif. Its persistence suggests that it is pointing at something; either a deeply rooted psychological archetype or a genuinely anomalous physical feature that multiple observers have independently attempted to describe.

The Hide That Cannot Be Pierced

The second distinguishing detail is the creature's alleged invulnerability. Indigenous accounts frequently state that the Mapinguari cannot be killed by conventional means. Arrows do not penetrate its hide. In more modern accounts, bullets are said to have no effect. This has been attributed, in the more scientifically inclined interpretations, to the creature's thick, matted fur acting as a kind of natural armor; a description that, as we shall see, has a startling parallel in the fossil record.

The layered defense system described; dense, matted fur over what appears to be an unusually tough hide, is consistent with what paleontologists know about the integumentary system of certain ground sloth species. *Mylodon darwinii*, the giant ground sloth whose preserved hide was famously recovered from a cave in Patagonia in the late nineteenth century, possessed skin embedded with thousands of small, bony nodules called osteoderms. These were not external plates like the armor of an armadillo. They were embedded within the dermis itself; a subdermal chainmail that would have made the animal's hide extraordinarily resistant to the teeth and claws of predators.

A surviving descendant species retaining this osteoderm structure, overlaid with the thick, matted fur described in witness accounts, would present a body surface that conventional projectiles; particularly the low-velocity arrows and small-caliber firearms available in the rural Amazon, might genuinely fail to penetrate. The invulnerability motif, which sounds supernatural on its face, may in fact be one of the most straightforward physical details in the entire Mapinguari tradition.

The Ground Sloth Hypothesis

It is the fossil record that elevates the Mapinguari from regional legend to a subject of genuine scientific curiosity.

The Amazon Basin was, until the end of the Pleistocene epoch roughly eleven thousand years ago, home to the giant ground sloths; a family of massive, herbivorous mammals that included species such as *Megatherium*, *Mylodon*, and *Eremotherium*. These were not the small, languid tree-dwellers of the modern tropics. They were titans. *Megatherium americanum* reached up to twenty feet in length and weighed several tons. *Eremotherium laurillardi*, the most common South American species, was similarly enormous. These animals walked on their hind legs when browsing. They were covered in thick fur. And their skin contained osteoderms; embedded dermal armor that would have made their hide extraordinarily resistant to penetration. The parallels between the paleontological record and the Mapinguari testimony are difficult to ignore. A large, fur-covered creature that walks upright, inhabits the deep forest, possesses a hide that resists penetration, bears large claws, and is found in the same geographical region where giant ground sloths were among the dominant megafauna for millions of years. The convergence is specific enough to warrant serious consideration.

David Oren, during his years of fieldwork in the Amazon, became increasingly convinced that the Mapinguari accounts were consistent with a surviving ground sloth. Oren was not a fringe enthusiast. He was a trained ornithologist with a doctoral degree from Harvard, working under the auspices of the Goeldi Museum in Belém, one of Brazil's most respected natural history institutions. His decision to pursue the Mapinguari question publicly was made with full awareness of the professional risk involved; a risk that, as the previous chapter's account of Grover Krantz illustrates, is not trivial.

Oren conducted extensive interviews with indigenous hunters and rubber tappers, many of whom described encountering the creature with a level of detail and emotional weight that he found impossible to dismiss as simple mythology. Several of his informants were experienced woodsmen who could identify every known animal in their territory by sight, sound, and track, and who insisted that the Mapinguari was something outside that catalogue entirely. Oren noted that the physical descriptions he collected; the reddish fur, the powerful build, the upright posture, the apparent hide armor, and the overwhelming stench, aligned more closely with what is known of the giant ground sloths than with any living animal.

Oren organized multiple expeditions into the deep forest in search of physical evidence. He collected hair samples, scat samples, and plaster casts of tracks from areas of reported activity. The results were inconclusive; the hair samples could not be definitively attributed to an unknown species, and the tracks, while unusual, did not provide the kind of unambiguous evidence required for formal taxonomic recognition. But the failure to find definitive proof is not the same as finding definitive disproof, and Oren's methodological approach; treating the Mapinguari as a zoological hypothesis to be tested rather than a legend to be debunked; remains a model for how this kind of inquiry should be conducted.

The ground sloth hypothesis also provides a framework for understanding the Mapinguari's reported behavior. Ground sloths were herbivores, but their size and natural armor would have made them formidable when threatened. A surviving species, adapted over millennia to the dense rainforest environment, might well have developed the kind of defensive behaviors described in the accounts; the territorial roaring, the overwhelming musk, the aggressive posturing toward anything perceived as a threat. These are not the behaviors of a predator. They are the behaviors of a large, powerful animal that would rather be left alone.

What the Forest Feeds

If the Mapinguari is a surviving ground sloth or a descendant of one, the question of diet becomes both tractable and important.

The extinct ground sloths were herbivores. Isotopic analysis of *Megatherium* bones and preserved *Mylodon* dung from Patagonian caves confirms a diet of grasses, shrubs, and tree foliage, with some evidence of selective browsing on specific plant species. A surviving Amazonian descendant, reduced in size from its Pleistocene ancestors but retaining the basic ground sloth body plan, would likely depend on the forest's substantial vegetative resources, leaves, fruits, tubers, roots, and the soft inner bark of certain tree species.

The Amazon provides this in abundance. The *terra firme* forests where Mapinguari sightings concentrate are among the most botanically diverse ecosystems on Earth, with hundreds of tree species per hectare and a year-round supply of fruit and foliage. A large herbivore with the powerful forelimbs and curved claws described in witness accounts would be well-equipped to access food sources that are unavailable to smaller browsers; tearing open rotting logs for grubs and fungi, stripping bark from tree trunks, and pulling down branches that are out of reach for ground-level feeders.

Several indigenous accounts describe the Mapinguari feeding on specific plants, particularly palms and their fruits. This is a noteworthy detail, because it is precisely the kind of ecological specificity that would be absent from a purely invented creature but present in accounts based on real observation. A storyteller invents a monster. A witness reports what the animal was eating.

The dietary question connects directly to the ecological feasibility analysis that later chapters will pursue. A large-bodied herbivore in the Amazon would require a substantial daily caloric intake; likely in the range of thirty to fifty pounds of plant material per day, depending on body mass and metabolic rate. The forest can easily supply this. The question is whether a population large enough to sustain a breeding population could feed itself in the available habitat without producing obvious signs of its presence, stripped trees, trampled vegetation, concentrated dung deposits. In a forest of this scale and density, the answer is more plausible than it might initially seem.

Traces in the Mud

The physical evidence associated with the Mapinguari is sparse; far sparser than the Bigfoot evidence base discussed in the previous chapter. This scarcity is itself a data point that requires interpretation rather than dismissal.

The Amazon presents unique challenges for evidence preservation. Tropical heat and humidity accelerate decomposition at rates that make temperate forests seem almost archival by comparison. A footprint in Amazonian mud can be erased by a single rainstorm, and rainstorms in the basin are not occasional events but near-daily occurrences for much of the year. Hair, scat, and other biological traces decompose rapidly. Bones are consumed by the forest floor's relentless recycling of organic material. The very conditions that make the Amazon a plausible refuge for an undiscovered large animal also make it extraordinarily difficult to collect and preserve the evidence that would confirm its existence.

That said, the evidence base is not entirely empty. Oren and other researchers collected track impressions from areas of reported Mapinguari activity. The tracks described are large; significantly larger than a human footprint, and display features that do not match any known Amazonian wildlife. The most consistent descriptions reference a rounded, somewhat elongated print with apparent claw marks at the leading edge, a morphology that is broadly consistent with ground sloth foot anatomy but inconsistent with the tracks of tapirs, jaguars, or any other large animal native to the region.

Hair samples collected from reported encounter sites have been subjected to microscopic analysis, with mixed results. Some samples have been identified as belonging to known species. Others have been classified as unidentifiable; not matching any species in the reference databases available to the analysts. This is suggestive but far from conclusive, particularly given the vast number of mammalian species in the Amazon that are poorly represented in forensic hair databases. No confirmed scat, bones, or tissue samples attributable to the Mapinguari have been recovered. This is the central evidentiary gap, and it is a significant one. But it is worth noting that the same gap existed for numerous confirmed species before their formal discovery; the saola, the giant forest hog, and the kipunji monkey were all known from indigenous testimony long before any physical specimen reached a laboratory. In the Amazon specifically, new mammal species continue to be described at a rate of several per decade, and the total number of undocumented species in the basin is estimated to be substantial. The absence of a type specimen does not close the question. It defines the question's current boundary.

Megafaunal Survival in the Amazon Basin

The assumption that large Ice Age fauna vanished entirely at the Pleistocene-Holocene boundary is increasingly nuanced. While most megafauna did disappear approximately eleven thousand years ago, the timing, pace, and completeness of those extinctions remain subjects of active scientific debate. Human overhunting, rapid climate fluctuation, and ecological cascade likely all played roles, and their relative contributions varied by region and by species. In South America, where the megafaunal extinction was among the most severe on any continent; eliminating ground sloths, glyptodonts, toxodonts, and dozens of other large-bodied species; the conventional narrative holds that nothing of significant size survived into the Holocene.

But conventional narratives have been wrong before, and the Amazon Basin presents a set of conditions that complicate the picture.

Unlike open plains ecosystems, where large animals are visible and vulnerable, dense tropical rainforests present a mosaic of microhabitats, river barriers, and isolation zones where small populations can persist with remarkably low density requirements. The Amazon's river systems: some of them miles wide, seasonally flooding areas the size of European nations; create natural barriers to dispersal that can isolate populations for thousands of generations. Within the *terra firme* forests between these rivers, conditions are stable enough to support resident megafauna but remote enough to preclude systematic survey by modern science. As of this writing, vast areas of the western Amazon have never been surveyed by mammalogists on foot.

The ecological capacity is there. Population viability models for large herbivores suggest that a breeding base of several hundred individuals dispersed across millions of hectares could remain genetically stable and largely undetected, provided the species is behaviorally nocturnal, territorially conservative, and occupies habitat that humans rarely penetrate. All three conditions are consistent with the Mapinguari accounts.

Consider the precedents. The coelacanth: a fish believed extinct for sixty-five million years, was rediscovered alive in 1938. The okapi, a large forest ungulate, was known to Central African pygmies for centuries before Western science confirmed it in 1901. The Chacoan peccary, a large pig-like mammal, was described from Pleistocene fossils and assumed extinct until living specimens were found in the Paraguayan Chaco in 1975. In the Amazon itself, the white-cheeked spider monkey, the Mura's saddleback tamarin, and several other primate species have been described to science only in the twenty-first century. These are not microorganisms or deep-sea invertebrates. They are large-bodied mammals living in a forest that continues to yield species that were previously unknown.

None of this proves that a ground sloth descendant survives in the Amazon today. But it moves the hypothesis from the realm of mythology into the realm of ecological feasibility; a distinction that matters enormously for how the question is pursued.

When the Forest Is Darkest

The temporal patterns of Mapinguari encounters, though less systematically documented than those of Bigfoot sightings, reveal a consistent tendency: the creature is most often encountered during the transitional hours of dawn and dusk, and a significant number of the most detailed accounts describe encounters that occurred in conditions of deep shade or near-darkness.

This is consistent with crepuscular or nocturnal activity; a behavioral pattern that would make biological sense for a large animal seeking to avoid both the midday heat of the tropical forest and the diurnal activity patterns of human hunters. Many of the Amazon's large mammals, including tapirs and jaguars, are primarily active during twilight and nighttime hours. A large, reclusive herbivore inhabiting the same ecosystem would face similar thermoregulatory and predator-avoidance pressures, and a shift toward low-light activity would be an expected adaptation.

The low-light encounter pattern also helps explain the relative vagueness of facial and fine anatomical descriptions in the Mapinguari accounts compared to those of Bigfoot. In the dense Amazonian understory, where even midday light is filtered through multiple layers of canopy, a creature encountered at dusk or dawn would be visible primarily as a silhouette; a massive, dark shape whose gross proportions and movement are discernible but whose detailed features are not. This is, in fact, exactly what most witnesses describe: an impression of size, shape, and wrongness rather than a detailed anatomical portrait.

The implications for evidence collection are significant. Camera traps deployed in Mapinguari research areas would need to be optimized for low-light conditions and positioned not on game trails, which the creature, like Bigfoot, may actively avoid, but in areas of reported territorial activity, near food sources, or along the natural corridors between *terra firme* forest blocks.

The Shaman's Warning

There is a dimension of the Mapinguari tradition that cannot be neatly filed under the heading of zoology, and it would be dishonest to omit it. For many of the indigenous cultures that speak of this creature, the Mapinguari is not simply an animal. It is something more; something that occupies a territory between the physical and the spiritual, and that carries with it a weight of meaning that transcends the merely biological.

In several Amazonian traditions, the Mapinguari is described as a transformed being. The most common version of this narrative holds that it was once a shaman; a man of considerable spiritual power who abused his gifts or violated a sacred law and was, as punishment, transformed into the creature. In this telling, the Mapinguari's rage, its territoriality, and its avoidance of humanity are not instinctual animal behaviors but the expressions of a cursed intelligence; a being that remembers what it was and suffers for what it has become.

This interpretation carries an element that is particularly unsettling: the suggestion of consciousness. An animal can be feared and respected. A creature that was once human, that retains some fragment of awareness within its monstrous form, evokes something deeper; a horror that touches on questions of identity, punishment, and the fragility of the boundary between the human and the inhuman. The Mapinguari, in this reading, is not a thing to be hunted or catalogued. It is a warning. It is the shape that waits at the end of transgression.

The Mouth That Should Not Be There

The most disturbing physical detail to emerge from the supernatural accounts is the creature's alleged second mouth. Located on its abdomen or chest, this secondary opening is described in some accounts as being capable of consuming food or, more ominously, as being the source of the creature's terrible roar. The image is grotesque and deliberately so; it transforms the body into something wrong, something that violates the basic template of mammalian anatomy in a way designed to inspire not just fear but revulsion.

Whether this detail originated as a literal observation, a symbolic embellishment, or a cultural artifact that accrued to the legend over generations is impossible to determine with certainty. But several interpretations deserve consideration.

The first is purely symbolic. A mouth in the belly is an ancient and widespread motif in world mythology, representing insatiable appetite, moral corruption, or the inversion of natural order. Its presence in the Mapinguari tradition may serve a narrative function; marking the creature as fundamentally *wrong*, as something that has crossed a boundary that should not be crossed, rather than describing an observed anatomical feature.

The second interpretation is more speculative but grounded in biology. Large mammals with ventral scent glands; glands located on the chest or abdomen, can produce openings or pouches in the skin that, to an observer unfamiliar with the anatomy, might appear mouth-like, particularly when the gland is actively secreting and the surrounding tissue is inflamed or distended. If the Mapinguari's overwhelming odor is produced by such a gland, and if that gland is located on the ventral surface of the body, a witness catching a brief, terrified glimpse of the creature could plausibly misidentify the structure as a second mouth. The association of the "mouth" with the creature's roar could be a secondary interpretation; the observer, having seen what appeared to be an opening on the creature's torso, attributing the sound to that opening rather than to the actual oral cavity.

The third possibility is that the second mouth is a conflation; a detail imported from the *Curupira* tradition or another Amazonian spiritual narrative and fused with the Mapinguari account over time. Cultural contamination of this kind is common in oral traditions, particularly when different communities describe creatures that share some characteristics but not others. Distinguishing the zoological signal from the mythological noise is one of the central challenges of Mapinguari research, and the second mouth is perhaps the clearest example of why that distinction matters.

The Sacred Boundary

The Mapinguari's rumored invulnerability, already discussed in its potential biological context, takes on additional meaning within the spiritual framework. If the creature is a cursed being, a transformed shaman, then its resistance to physical harm is not a matter of thick skin or bony armor. It is a mark of its supernatural nature; a sign that it exists partially outside the laws that govern ordinary flesh. This is a common motif in world mythology: the cursed being that cannot be easily destroyed, the monster that must be dealt with through spiritual means rather than brute force.

It would be a mistake to dismiss these supernatural elements as mere superstition layered onto an otherwise zoological phenomenon. For the cultures that produced and maintain these traditions, the spiritual and the physical are not separate categories. The forest is not simply a collection of trees and animals; it is a living system with its own intelligence, its own rules, and its own enforcers. The Mapinguari, whether it is a surviving ground sloth, a transformed shaman, or something that partakes of both realities simultaneously, serves a function within this system. It is the guardian of the deep places, the consequence of going too far, the reminder that there are parts of the world that belong to something other than humanity.

The shaman's warning, in the end, may be the most important part of the Mapinguari tradition; not because it proves or disproves the creature's physical existence, but because it illuminates the relationship between a culture and its landscape. A relationship in which the unknown is not simply a gap in knowledge to be filled, but a necessary and sacred boundary to be respected.

This dual nature: the creature as both zoological possibility and spiritual boundary marker, is something the comparative chapters of this book will return to, because it is not unique to the Mapinguari. The same pattern, with different cultural clothing, appears in the Aboriginal traditions surrounding the Yowie and in certain indigenous perspectives on the Sasquatch. The question of what it means when a creature serves both a biological and a spiritual function is not a question zoology can answer alone. But it is a question this book cannot afford to ignore.

Case Study: The Hunter Who Would Not Return

In the late twentieth century, reports collected by researchers including David Oren included recurring testimony from rubber tappers and indigenous hunters operating in the western Brazilian Amazon. One account, repeated in varying forms across multiple communities, tells of a hunter who ventured too deep into the forest during the dry season.

The man was experienced. He knew the territory, the seasonal water levels, and the signs of every known animal in the region. On the third day of his excursion, he reportedly detected a powerful stench; far stronger than that of any carcass or territorial mammal he had encountered before. The smell was described as nauseating, metallic, and suffocating.

Moments later, according to the account, he heard a roar.

The roar was not sharp like a jaguar nor rising like a howler monkey. It was sustained; a deep, resonant bellow that seemed to vibrate through the forest floor itself. The man dropped his equipment and fled, describing the sensation as one of primal dread rather than calculated fear.

He reportedly glanced back once and saw a large, fur-covered figure partially obscured by trees. The proportions were wrong; too thick through the torso, too upright to be any known animal. He did not observe details of the face. The smell intensified before abruptly dissipating.

When he returned to his village, he reportedly refused to revisit the region. Elders interpreted the event as a Mapinguari warning, an enforcement of the boundary between human foraging territory and the sacred deep forest. The hunter did not vanish. He was not physically harmed. But he did not return to that section of forest again.

From a zoological standpoint, the most notable elements are the smell, the roar, and the behavioral pattern. No attack. No pursuit over distance. A territorial display sufficient to drive the intruder out, and nothing more. Whether interpreted as surviving megafauna or spiritual enforcement, the pattern aligns remarkably well with defensive behavior observed in large herbivores globally. Elephants trumpet and charge to drive intruders from their territory, then break off pursuit once the threat has retreated. Rhinoceroses make bluff charges. Hippopotamuses bellow. The warning is the point. Contact beyond that is unnecessary.

The hunter's account, like so many in the Mapinguari record, ends not with a dramatic confrontation but with an absence; the creature withdrawing, the smell fading, the forest closing behind it as though nothing had happened. It is the recurring signature of a phenomenon that does not seek human attention. It seeks the opposite.

The Deepest Interior

The Mapinguari, more than perhaps any other cryptid examined in this series, is defined by its habitat. The creature and the Amazon are inseparable; not only because the forest provides the concealment that makes the creature's hypothetical survival possible, but because the forest itself is the context that gives the accounts their weight.

In the Pacific Northwest, Bigfoot is reported from wilderness areas that are, by Amazonian standards, thoroughly explored. There are roads, trails, logging access routes, and satellite coverage that leaves few areas genuinely unsurveyed. The Amazon offers no such infrastructure. The deep *terra firme* forests between the major river systems remain, in many cases, as unknown to modern science as they were a century ago. Satellite imagery reveals the canopy. It reveals nothing of what moves beneath it.

This is not a permanent condition. Deforestation, roadbuilding, and the expansion of agricultural frontiers are eating into the Amazon at a pace that makes the window for discovery, if there is anything to discover, a narrowing one. The same isolation that may have protected a relic population for thousands of years is being eroded by the chainsaw and the bulldozer. If the Mapinguari exists, the forest it depends on is disappearing.

The irony is bitter but worth stating plainly: the creature most likely to be real among the cryptids in this book is also the one whose habitat is most immediately threatened. The question may not be whether the Mapinguari can be found. It may be whether the Mapinguari can survive long enough to be looked for.

In the next chapter, we leave the twilight of the Amazon canopy for the eucalyptus forests and sandstone gorges of Australia, where the oldest continuous culture on Earth has its own name for the thing that watches from the tree line. The Yowie has waited a very long time to be taken seriously. Its turn has come.

Chapter 3: The Yowie — The Guardian of the Outback

The Burley-Dush

Australia is a continent defined by its strangeness. Separated from the rest of the world's landmasses for tens of millions of years, it evolved in isolation, producing an ecosystem that operates on fundamentally different rules than those found elsewhere on Earth. Marsupials replaced placental mammals. Monotremes: egg-laying mammals that vanished from other continents, persisted and thrived. The reptiles grew larger. The birds grew deadlier. The trees shed their bark instead of their leaves. Nothing about Australia's biology follows the template established on other landmasses, and this fact is not incidental to the chapter that follows. It is central to it.

Because if a large, hair-covered, bipedal creature exists in the forests of Australia, it exists in a place where no such creature should be possible. There are no native apes on the Australian continent. There are no native monkeys. There is no fossil record of any primate; not one, in the entire geological history of Australia since its separation from Gondwana. Whatever the Yowie is, if it is anything at all, it represents either an impossibility or a mystery of a different order than Bigfoot or the Mapinguari. It is the hardest case in this book, and for that reason, the most interesting one.

The Aboriginal peoples of Australia are the custodians of the oldest continuous culture on Earth, with an unbroken history stretching back at least sixty thousand years; and possibly longer. To put that span in perspective: when the ancestors of today's Aboriginal Australians were already established on this continent, the Neanderthals had not yet disappeared from Europe, the last glacial maximum had not yet begun, and the entire arc of what we call human civilization; agriculture, writing, cities, empires, lay tens of thousands of years in the future. These are people whose cultural memory extends into a depth of time that most modern minds cannot meaningfully comprehend.

Their Dreamtime traditions: the vast, interconnected body of narrative that explains the creation and ongoing nature of the world, contain references to large, hairy, humanlike beings that have been a recognized part of the Australian landscape for as long as anyone can remember. The names vary by nation and by region. In the Sydney basin and the Blue Mountains, the creature was known to the Dharug and Gundungurra peoples. In Queensland, the Kuku Yalanji spoke of beings in the tropical rainforests of the Daintree. The Bundjalung people of the Northern Rivers region used their own names. Across the continent, the terms include Yowie, Yahoo, Doolagahl, Joogabinna, Gulaga, and Burley-Dush; this last carrying a particular sense of menace.

The diversity of names matters, because it reflects the diversity of the source. These are not variations on a single story that migrated from one nation to the next. Aboriginal Australia comprised hundreds of distinct language groups, many of which had limited contact with one another and maintained independent oral traditions over periods that dwarf the recorded history of any other civilization. When dozens of these independent traditions describe the same kind of creature; large, hairy, bipedal, aggressive, inhabiting the deep forest, the convergence cannot be comfortably explained as cultural diffusion. It is either a shared psychological archetype expressed through similar ecological conditions, or it is a shared observation of something that was actually there.

Ecological Memory and the Dreamtime

There is growing scientific recognition that Aboriginal oral traditions encode genuine ecological information of extraordinary antiquity. Research published in the twenty-first century has demonstrated that Dreamtime narratives contain accurate descriptions of sea-level changes, volcanic eruptions, and megafaunal extinctions that occurred thousands of years ago; events confirmed by geological evidence but preserved in no written record. These are not vague mythological references. They are specific, geographically anchored accounts that have been transmitted with remarkable fidelity across hundreds of generations.

This has profound implications for how we approach the Yowie traditions. If Aboriginal oral history reliably preserves information about coastlines that were drowned ten thousand years ago, about volcanoes that erupted seven thousand years ago, and about giant animals that disappeared from the landscape forty-six thousand years ago, then the possibility that it also preserves information about a large, bipedal creature that coexisted with Aboriginal peoples cannot be dismissed on the grounds that oral tradition is inherently unreliable. The track record suggests the opposite.

The Dreamtime accounts describe these beings as inhabiting the dense forests, mountain ranges, and deep gorges of the Australian landscape. They are large, powerful, covered in hair, and decidedly not friendly. Unlike the Sasquatch, which is more often described as elusive and avoidant, the hairy beings of Aboriginal tradition are frequently characterized as aggressive; willing to confront, chase, and in some accounts, harm those who enter their territory. This behavioral distinction is one of the defining features of the Australian tradition and sets it apart from its Northern Hemisphere counterparts in important ways that the comparative chapters will examine.

First Contacts: The Colonial Record

The arrival of European colonists in the late eighteenth century brought a new set of eyes to the Australian landscape and, almost immediately, a new set of encounters.

Early colonial records from the late 1700s and early 1800s contain scattered but persistent references to large, apelike creatures observed in the bush by settlers, convicts, and explorers. These accounts are notable for their lack of sensationalism. They appear in journals, letters, and official reports as straightforward descriptions of something seen and not understood. The witnesses were, in many cases, men who had no knowledge of Aboriginal tradition and no framework for interpreting what they encountered other than their own European experience; which, critically, included no native apes or large primates of any kind. The British Isles, from which the majority of early colonists came, had no cultural equivalent to the Sasquatch or the Yowie. These men had no template for what they were reporting, and that absence of expectation lends their accounts a particular credibility.

Among the earliest documented accounts is a report from 1795 in which a party near Sydney described observing a large, dark, manlike figure moving through the bush on two legs. The account was noted in colonial records without elaboration; a detail mentioned alongside observations about weather, terrain, and local wildlife, as though the writer considered it merely another feature of an unfamiliar landscape. In subsequent decades, similar accounts accumulated from settlers pushing into the Blue Mountains, the Hunter Valley, and the forested ranges north and south of Sydney.

The 1800s produced a steady stream of reports that were covered, with varying degrees of seriousness, in colonial and regional newspapers. The *Sydney Morning Herald*, the *Australian Town and Country Journal*, and numerous regional papers published accounts of encounters with "wild men" or "ape-like creatures" in the bush. These press accounts are valuable not because they represent rigorous investigation; they do not, but because they establish that the phenomenon was being reported by European Australians independently of Aboriginal tradition, and that it was being reported with enough frequency to warrant repeated coverage.

The colonial accounts describe a creature that stood between five and eight feet tall; somewhat shorter, on average, than the North American Bigfoot, with a heavily muscled, stocky build and a covering of dark hair. The face was described as broad and somewhat flattened, and the overall impression was frequently compared to a large ape or, in the language of the time, a "wild man." Several accounts note that the creatures were seen in pairs or small groups, suggesting a social structure of some kind; a detail that aligns with Aboriginal traditions describing the creatures as living in family units rather than as solitary individuals.

The convergence of indigenous tradition and colonial observation creates a historical record that, while fragmentary, is difficult to explain away as simple misidentification or cultural transmission. The Aboriginal accounts predate European contact by millennia. The colonial accounts were produced by men who, in most cases, had no awareness of the Aboriginal traditions. The fact that both sets of observers, separated by an immense gulf of time and culture, described fundamentally the same thing is a coincidence that strains the limits of coincidence.

The Map of the Yowie

The name "Yowie" itself appears to derive from an Aboriginal word, though its exact linguistic origin is debated. It entered common usage in European-Australian culture during the nineteenth century and has remained the dominant term ever since. But to understand the creature, it is necessary to understand where it is reported, and where it is not. The popular imagination, to the extent that it considers the Yowie at all, tends to place it in the Blue Mountains west of Sydney. This is understandable; the Blue Mountains are the most concentrated and best-documented hotspot for Yowie activity in Australia, and they will receive detailed treatment later in this chapter. But the Yowie is not a Blue Mountains phenomenon any more than Bigfoot is a Pacific Northwest phenomenon. The geographic range of reported encounters spans the entire eastern seaboard of the continent and extends into regions that rarely feature in the popular narrative.

The Gold Coast hinterland and the Springbrook Plateau in southeastern Queensland have produced a substantial body of sighting reports, particularly from the rainforest-clad mountains that rise steeply behind the coastal strip. The D'Aguilar Range north of

Brisbane, the Bunya Mountains further west, and the dense tropical rainforests of the Atherton Tablelands in Far North Queensland all contribute reports. In New South Wales, beyond the Blue Mountains, the Barrington Tops wilderness area, the Pilliga Forest in the state's northwest, the Watagan Mountains south of Newcastle, and the forested escarpments of the South Coast have all generated encounters. Reports extend into Victoria, into the Otway Ranges and the forests of Gippsland, and into the remote wilderness areas of Tasmania.

The pattern that emerges from this geographic spread is consistent and suggestive. Yowie reports concentrate in areas of dense forest cover, rugged terrain, reliable water supply, and limited human access. They cluster along the Great Dividing Range; the mountain spine that runs the length of eastern Australia, and in the pockets of rainforest, wet sclerophyll forest, and deep gorge country that the Range supports. The creature, if it exists, is not randomly distributed. It is distributed in exactly the pattern that a large, forest-dependent animal would occupy: continuous or semi-continuous habitat corridors running along the eastern ranges, with population concentrations in areas of particular ecological richness.

This distribution also correlates with the distribution of Australia's surviving large fauna. The eastern forests are where the greatest concentrations of kangaroos, wombats, possums, and other large marsupials are found. They are where the most intact forest ecosystems remain. And they are where, not coincidentally, Aboriginal traditions about the Yowie are most detailed and most persistent.

The Aggressive Ape

If the Bigfoot of North America is often characterized as the gentle giant; a creature that flees from human contact and wishes only to be left alone, then the Yowie is its temperamental opposite. The behavioral profile that emerges from the accumulated testimony paints a picture of a creature that is, by the standards of its fellow hairy humanoids, remarkably confrontational.

Country Cousins: Bigfoot, Mapinguari and the Yowie

Witnesses do not simply report seeing the Yowie at a distance and watching it retreat. They report being approached. They report being followed. They report standing in their kitchens or on their porches and realizing that something enormous and covered in hair is standing in their yard, staring at them through the window with an intensity that goes beyond animal curiosity. In numerous accounts, the Yowie does not flee when discovered. It holds its ground. It advances. In some cases, it charges.

This behavioral pattern has been consistent across decades of reports, from rural New South Wales to the tropical forests of Queensland to the rugged bushland of the Blue Mountains. Witnesses who have had close encounters describe a creature that is not merely unafraid of humans but seems to regard them as intruders; territorial violations to be met with aggression rather than avoidance. The emotional tenor of Yowie encounter reports is qualitatively different from the typical Bigfoot account. Where Bigfoot witnesses often describe awe, wonder, or a kind of reverent fear, Yowie witnesses far more frequently describe a raw, immediate terror; the fear of being in the presence of something that might attack.

The physical build described in these encounters is consistent with this more aggressive profile. The Yowie is typically reported as shorter but considerably stockier than the North American Bigfoot; broader through the chest and shoulders, more heavily muscled, with a build that has been compared most often to that of a gorilla. The head is large and sits low on the shoulders, and the brow ridge is pronounced. The overall impression is one of compressed, concentrated power; a body built not for the long-distance, ground-covering locomotion of the Bigfoot but for short bursts of explosive strength.

There is a paradox at the heart of the Yowie's aggressiveness, however. Despite the numerous accounts of confrontational behavior, the charges, the displays, the terrifying vocalizations, there are no confirmed accounts of a Yowie physically attacking and injuring a human being. The aggression, fearsome as it is, appears to be primarily performative; a set of warning behaviors designed to drive intruders away rather than to inflict actual harm. This is, again, consistent with the behavior of known great apes, which engage in elaborate and frightening threat displays that very rarely escalate to actual violence. The goal is deterrence, not combat. The Yowie, it seems, wants you gone. It does not necessarily want you dead.

The Ethology of Intimidation

The distinction between performative aggression and predatory aggression is well-established in primate ethology, and it provides a useful framework for interpreting the Yowie behavioral data. Chimpanzees, gorillas, and even smaller primate species engage in dramatic threat displays: charging, branch shaking, ground pounding, and loud vocalizations. These displays are energetically expensive and rarely escalate to lethal attack. Their purpose is deterrence without injury; a way of enforcing territorial boundaries and establishing dominance hierarchies without the risks that accompany actual combat. The pattern is so consistent across primate species that it can reasonably be called a primate universal.

The Yowie behavioral pattern: advance, vocalize, strike nearby vegetation, hold ground, retreat, aligns closely with this ethological template. If the Yowie is a primate, its aggression is not anomalous. It is typical. What makes it appear anomalous is the comparison to Bigfoot, which is most often described as avoidant. But avoidance and confrontation are not opposing strategies in primate behavior; they are context-dependent responses that the same species can deploy depending on circumstances. A creature that avoids humans in the vast, low-density wilderness of the Pacific Northwest might confront them in the more compressed, fragmented habitat of the Australian eastern ranges, where encounters occur at closer quarters and retreat options are more limited.

This ecological interpretation of the behavioral difference; avoidance where space permits, confrontation where it does not, is one of the more productive insights the comparative method generates, and the later chapters will examine it in detail.

The Stench of the Bush

The smell associated with Yowie encounters has received less systematic attention than its North American and South American counterparts, but it is present in the record and consistent enough to warrant examination.

Witnesses who have been in close proximity to the creature describe a powerful, unpleasant odor; most commonly compared to a strong animal musk, wet fur, or decaying organic matter. The descriptions are less extreme than those associated with the Mapinguari, whose stench is reported as incapacitating, and more closely aligned with the Bigfoot odor in both character and intensity. Several Blue Mountains witnesses have described the smell as similar to a wet dog multiplied many times over, with an underlying sharpness that one account compared to ammonia.

The smell is not reported in every Yowie encounter, which may reflect distance, wind conditions, or individual variation; or may indicate that scent production is context-dependent, intensifying during periods of stress or territorial assertion. In the great apes, odor production is known to increase during states of emotional arousal. A silverback gorilla in a state of agitation produces noticeably more scent than one at rest. If the Yowie follows a similar pattern, the encounters most likely to include a smell component would be precisely the confrontational, high-arousal encounters that dominate the Australian record; which is, in fact, what the data suggests.

The three-way comparison is worth marking explicitly here. All three creatures examined in this book; Bigfoot, the Mapinguari, and the Yowie, are associated with a powerful biological odor. The character of the odor varies in ways that may reflect differences in diet, habitat, or glandular physiology. The Mapinguari's stench is the most extreme, possibly reflecting an adaptation to chemical communication in the low-visibility Amazon understory. The Bigfoot odor is strong but less frequently described as incapacitating. The Yowie odor falls in a similar range to Bigfoot's. This gradient: from overwhelming to strong to moderate, may correlate with the density of the habitat and the degree to which each creature relies on chemical rather than visual signaling. Or it may simply reflect differences in the witness populations' frames of reference. The comparative chapters will untangle this further.

Red Eyes in the Dark

The eyes are another frequently noted feature, and here the Yowie diverges sharply from its counterparts in ways that demand attention. Multiple witnesses have reported that the creature's eyes appear to glow red in low light or darkness; a detail that is consistent across enough independent reports to constitute a genuine pattern rather than a recurring embellishment. The color is described not as a reflection of ambient light but as an apparent self-luminescence: a deep, steady red glow visible even in conditions where no obvious light source is available to produce a reflective eye shine.

This requires careful parsing. Eye shine: the reflection of light from the tapetum lucidum, is well-established zoological phenomenon, found in a wide range of nocturnal and crepuscular animals. The color of the eye shine varies by species and depends on the structure of the tapetum: cats typically produce green or yellow eye shine, dogs produce green or blue, and some marsupials produce a distinctive red or orange reflection. If the Yowie possesses a tapetum lucidum; which its apparent preference for low-light activity would suggest, then eye shine in response to a flashlight, headlamp, or campfire would be entirely expected.

The reports of apparent self-luminescence; eyes glowing without an obvious external light source, are harder to explain through conventional biology. No known mammal produces bioluminescent eye glow. The most likely explanation is that witnesses are detecting tapetum-reflected light from sources they are not consciously aware of; moonlight, distant artificial light, or even starlight, which can be sufficient to produce faint eye shine in an animal with a highly reflective tapetum at close range. The perception of self-luminescence may be an artifact of the encounter conditions: darkness, fear, and the narrowing of attention that accompanies a high-stress event.

What is not in dispute is that the red eye reports are frequent, geographically distributed, and consistent in their description. They appear in accounts from the Blue Mountains, from Queensland, from the New South Wales south coast, and from Victoria. And they appear almost exclusively in nighttime or deep-twilight encounters, which brings us to the question of when the Yowie is active.

The nocturnal pattern in Australian Yowie reports is pronounced. The majority of close-range encounters occur after dark or during the transitional hours of dusk and dawn. Daytime sightings exist but are less common and typically occur at greater distance, as though the creature is more willing to tolerate proximity in darkness; when its visual advantage is greatest, than in daylight, when the advantage shifts to the human observer. This pattern is consistent with the nocturnal and crepuscular activity profiles of many Australian mammals, including several of the larger marsupials, and would represent a sensible adaptation for a large animal seeking to minimize contact with diurnal human activity.

The Biogeographic Problem

Any honest treatment of the Yowie must confront, directly and without evasion, the central challenge that separates it from every other cryptid in this book: Australia has no primates.

This is not a gap in the fossil record that might be filled by future discovery. It is a consequence of deep geological time. Australia separated from Antarctica approximately forty-five million years ago, completing its isolation from the other southern landmasses. By the time primates had diversified into the forms that would eventually produce the great apes, the monkeys, and the prosimians, Australia was already an island continent; surrounded by deep ocean, unreachable by any land bridge, and developing its own unique fauna in complete isolation. No primate has ever been found in the Australian fossil record. Not a tooth. Not a bone fragment. Not a trace. This poses an obvious and serious problem for any hypothesis that the Yowie is a surviving unknown primate. It is, in fact, the strongest single argument against the creature's existence, and it cannot be argued away with appeals to undiscovered fossil beds or gaps in paleontological sampling. The fossil record of Australian mammals is, by global standards, remarkably well-studied. If primates had been present at any point in the last forty-five million years, evidence of them would almost certainly have been found.

There are, however, several responses to this challenge that deserve consideration; not because any of them is conclusive, but because the biogeographic problem, while severe, is not necessarily terminal.

The first is the possibility of a relatively recent arrival. Australia was not always as isolated as it is today. During the Pleistocene ice ages, lowered sea levels exposed the continental shelf, creating a series of land bridges and short water crossings between Southeast Asia and Australia; the route that human beings themselves used to reach the continent at least sixty thousand years ago. If humans could cross, other species could as well. The fossil record shows that several Southeast Asian species reached Australia or its near-neighbor islands during the Pleistocene, including the giant stork *Leptoptilos robustus* and the pygmy proboscidean *Stegodon*. A primate species: even a large-bodied one, making a similar crossing is not outside the bounds of physical possibility, particularly if it was aided by the same land bridge and island-hopping conditions that facilitated human migration. If such a crossing occurred during the Pleistocene, the species would have had between sixty thousand and roughly fifteen thousand years; the window during which sea levels were low enough to permit crossings, to establish itself in Australia. This is a short span in evolutionary terms, which might explain the absence of fossil evidence: a geologically recent arrival that occupied densely forested habitats in a geographically limited range could plausibly leave a fossil footprint so faint as to be undetectable in the current sample.

The second possibility is more radical: that the Yowie is not a primate at all. Australia's evolutionary history has produced numerous examples of convergent evolution; instances where Australian species have independently evolved body plans and behaviors that closely resemble those of placental mammals on other continents. The thylacine evolved to resemble a wolf. The numbat resembles an anteater. The sugar glider resembles a flying squirrel. In every case, unrelated animals arrived at similar solutions to similar ecological problems.

Could a large, bipedal, hair-covered marsupial have evolved in Australia to fill a niche similar to the one occupied by great apes elsewhere? The idea sounds extraordinary, but it is not without a basis in Australian paleontology. The continent's megafaunal past included large, bipedal marsupials; most notably the giant short-faced kangaroos of the genus *Procoptodon*, which stood over six feet tall and walked with an upright, striding gait rather than hopping. There were also the marsupial "lions" (*Thylacoleo*) and enormous wombat relatives (*Diprotodon*) that demonstrate the capacity of Australian evolution to produce large-bodied, ecologically dominant marsupials of considerable diversity. A bipedal, forest-dwelling marsupial; evolved independently but convergent in appearance with the great apes; is speculative, but it is speculative within a framework that Australia's own evolutionary history has established.

The third possibility is the simplest: that the Yowie does not exist as a biological species, and that the reports are the product of misidentification, cultural tradition, and human psychology operating on a continent whose forests are genuinely strange enough to provoke encounters with the unknown. This explanation must remain on the table not as a dismissal but as a competing hypothesis to be weighed against the evidence.

The biogeographic problem does not close the door on the Yowie. But it does change the character of the investigation. Where Bigfoot can be discussed within the familiar framework of known primate evolution, and the Mapinguari can be connected to a documented fossil lineage, the Yowie demands either a more creative hypothesis or a higher bar of evidence. It is the case where the comparative method earns its keep, because only by placing the Yowie beside its counterparts can we see which features of the phenomenon survive the removal of a convenient evolutionary explanation, and what that survival implies.

Australia's Lost Giants

To understand the ecological context in which the Yowie exists; or is reported to exist, it is necessary to reckon with what Australia has already lost.

Approximately forty-six thousand years ago, shortly after the arrival of the first human populations, Australia underwent a megafaunal extinction of devastating scope. The continent lost more than eighty-five percent of its large-bodied animal species in a geological eyeblink. *Diprotodon optatum*, a wombat relative the size of a rhinoceros and the largest marsupial ever to have lived, vanished. *Thylacoleo carnifex*, the marsupial lion; a powerful, tree-climbing predator with shearing teeth and retractable claws, vanished. The giant short-faced kangaroos, the massive flightless birds, the enormous goannas, all gone. The ecosystem that Aboriginal Australians inherited was already a diminished one, stripped of the megafauna that had shaped it for millions of years.

The causes remain debated. Human hunting, landscape burning, and climate change have all been proposed, and the most current research suggests a combination of factors. What matters for the Yowie question is not why the megafauna disappeared, but what the extinction tells us about the landscape's capacity to support large animals, and about the reliability of Aboriginal oral tradition in recording their existence.

Because the Dreamtime traditions do record them. Aboriginal oral histories contain descriptions of giant animals that align with remarkable specificity to known megafaunal species; descriptions that were dismissed as mythology for decades until paleontological evidence confirmed that the animals described had actually existed. If Aboriginal oral tradition preserved accurate accounts of *Diprotodon* and *Thylacoleo* across forty-six thousand years, the tradition's accounts of a large, bipedal, hairy creature cannot be dismissed on the assumption that oral traditions do not preserve real information. They demonstrably do.

The megafaunal extinction also establishes that Australia's eastern forests; the very habitats where the Yowie is reported, once supported a diverse assemblage of large-bodied animals. The carrying capacity was there. The habitat was there. The question is whether any remnant of that vanished world might have persisted in the deep gorges and mountain forests that human activity has been slowest to transform.

Traces in the Leaf Litter

The physical evidence associated with the Yowie is thin; thinner than the Bigfoot evidence base and roughly comparable to that of the Mapinguari. This scarcity must be acknowledged honestly before it can be examined productively.

Footprints constitute the largest category of physical evidence. Yowie tracks have been reported and, in some cases, cast in plaster from sites across eastern Australia. The prints are typically described as large; fourteen to eighteen inches in length, and broadly humanoid in shape, with five toes and a heel impression. They lack the mid-tarsal break that Jeff Meldrum has identified in some Bigfoot casts, displaying instead a flatter, more rigid profile that some investigators have compared to a human foot scaled up significantly in size. The toe splay is wider than human norms, and the stride length, where measurable, exceeds what would be expected from a human of the implied foot size.

The quality and documentation of Yowie track evidence varies enormously. Some casts have been made under controlled conditions by investigators who recorded the site, measured stride length and depth, photographed the surrounding terrain, and preserved the casts for later analysis. Others have been cast by enthusiasts with limited training and no chain of custody. The result is an evidence base that contains potentially valuable specimens mixed with material of uncertain provenance; a problem that plagues cryptid research globally but is particularly acute in Australia, where the research community is smaller and less institutionally supported than its North American counterpart.

Hair samples have been collected from reported Yowie encounter sites and submitted for analysis on several occasions. The results, as with Mapinguari hair samples, have been inconclusive, some samples identified as belonging to known species, others classified as unidentifiable or, in a few cases, as "primate-like" by the analysts who examined them. The "primate-like" designation is more problematic in Australia than elsewhere, given the absence of native primates: any genuinely primate hair found in the Australian bush would be either contamination from a human source, an escapee from a zoo or private collection, or evidence of something genuinely anomalous. To date, no analysis has been rigorous enough to distinguish definitively among these possibilities.

Scat, nesting structures, and feeding traces have been reported from areas of Yowie activity but have not been subjected to the kind of systematic collection and laboratory analysis that would be required to draw meaningful conclusions. This is less a failure of the evidence than a failure of the investigation; a consequence of the institutional barriers and resource limitations that will be examined in a later chapter.

Environmental DNA sampling, which has begun to be deployed in Bigfoot research areas in North America, has not yet been systematically applied to Yowie habitats. Given the challenges of eDNA collection in warm, humid forest environments; where DNA degrades rapidly and the background biological signal is enormous, the technique may require significant methodological adaptation before it can be productively deployed in the Australian context. But it represents, as with the Mapinguari, the most promising technological frontier for a creature that has resisted every previous attempt at physical confirmation.

The Investigators

The serious investigation of the Yowie has been carried forward by a small, dedicated, and largely unrecognized community of researchers who have pursued the question with varying degrees of rigor and personal sacrifice.

Rex Gilroy, a self-taught naturalist based in the Blue Mountains, has been the most visible and prolific figure in Australian Yowie research for over five decades. Gilroy has collected hundreds of sighting reports, amassed a large collection of plaster track casts, and advanced a theory connecting the Yowie to *Gigantopithecus* or a related fossil ape that he believes crossed into Australia during the Pleistocene. His work is extensive and his dedication is beyond question, but his methodology has drawn criticism from both mainstream scientists and other cryptid researchers, and his broader claims; which extend into other areas of fringe archaeology, have complicated his credibility as a source on the Yowie specifically.

Tony Healy and Paul Cropper, co-authors of *The Yowie: In Search of Australia's Bigfoot*, produced what remains the most comprehensive and critically minded survey of the Australian evidence. Their work is notable for its refusal to advocate for a single explanation, presenting the sighting data, the indigenous traditions, and the physical evidence with a journalistic rigor that allows the reader to evaluate the material on its own merits. Healy and Cropper's book is the essential reference for any serious engagement with the subject and a model for how cryptid case literature should be written.

Gary Opit, a naturalist and environmental consultant based in northern New South Wales, has brought a trained ecologist's eye to the Yowie question. Opit's investigations have focused on habitat analysis, feeding ecology, and the correlation between sighting reports and specific environmental conditions. His approach: treating the Yowie as a wildlife management question rather than a mystery, represents the kind of methodological shift that the field most urgently needs.

Dean Harrison, founder of Australian Yowie Research, has accumulated one of the largest databases of firsthand sighting reports in Australia through decades of field investigation and witness interviews. Harrison's work emphasizes the experiential dimension of Yowie encounters; the psychological and emotional impact on witnesses, and his database provides a resource for the kind of statistical analysis that the phenomenon has rarely received.

These researchers, like their counterparts in the Bigfoot and Mapinguari fields, have worked largely without institutional support, without funding, and without the professional recognition that would accompany equivalent effort directed at a less controversial subject. Their work forms the foundation on which any future investigation must build.

What the Yowie Eats

The dietary question for the Yowie is simultaneously one of the most important and least addressed aspects of the phenomenon. Later chapters will model the ecological feasibility of hidden populations in each of the three habitats examined in this book, and those models require assumptions about caloric requirements, which in turn require assumptions about diet.

The Australian eastern forests provide a food base that differs significantly from the environments occupied by Bigfoot and the

Mapinguari. There are no salmon runs. There are no large tropical fruits. The dominant vegetation is eucalyptus; a genus that is, for most mammals, essentially inedible, its leaves laden with toxic oils and offering minimal nutritional value. The animals that do consume eucalyptus, most notably the koala, require highly specialized digestive systems and low metabolic rates that are incompatible with the large, active body plan described in Yowie reports.

A large omnivore in the Australian eastern forests would need to exploit different food sources. The most plausible candidates include the roots and tubers of forest-floor plants, the fruits of rainforest species in the subtropical and tropical sections of the range, the eggs and young of ground-nesting birds, small mammals and reptiles, freshwater crayfish and fish from the creek systems that run through the gorge country, and perhaps most importantly; the large populations of marsupials and macropods that share the same habitat. Kangaroos, wallabies, wombats, and possums represent a substantial and renewable protein base for any predator large and strong enough to catch them.

Several Yowie accounts describe the creature near water; along creek banks, at river crossings, and near waterholes, with sufficient frequency to suggest that waterways may be important features of its habitat use. Whether this reflects drinking behavior, fishing activity, or the simple fact that creek corridors serve as travel routes through rugged terrain is impossible to determine from the available data. But the pattern is consistent with the habitat use of many large Australian animals, which orient their movements around reliable water sources, particularly during the dry months.

The dietary profile that emerges; if we accept the premise of a large, active omnivore, is more similar to that of a bear than to that of any known primate. This is itself an interesting data point, because Australia has no bears and never has. Whatever ecological niche the Yowie occupies, it is a niche that no known Australian animal currently fills; a vacancy in the ecosystem that was left open by the megafaunal extinction and that, conceivably, has been filled by something that has no close relatives on the continent.

The Blue Mountains: Where the Wild Holds

West of Sydney, beyond the suburban sprawl and the commuter towns, the landscape buckles upward into a series of deep, forested gorges and sandstone plateaus known as the Blue Mountains. The name comes from the fine mist of eucalyptus oil released by the millions of trees that blanket the region, giving the air a faint blue haze when viewed from a distance. It is a landscape of startling beauty and surprising wildness; a place where, despite its proximity to a metropolitan area of five million people, the terrain remains rugged and the forests remain deep enough to harbor things that prefer not to be found.

The Blue Mountains have been a persistent hotspot for Yowie activity for well over a century. Reports from the region date back to the colonial period and have continued with remarkable regularity into the modern era. The density of sightings in this area has drawn investigators from across Australia, and the accumulated body of testimony constitutes one of the most concentrated collections of hairy humanoid encounter data anywhere in the world.

The typical Blue Mountains encounter follows a pattern that will, by now, feel familiar in its broad strokes but distinctive in its details. A bushwalker, a camper, or a rural resident notices something wrong. The first sign is often auditory; a heavy footfall in the undergrowth, a branch snapping with a force that implies considerable weight, or a vocalization that does not fit any known animal. Then comes the silence.

The Sound of Nothing

The Australian bush is never silent. It is, under normal circumstances, a wall of sound, the calls of kookaburras, cockatoos, and currawongs, the buzzing of insects, the rustling of possums and wallabies in the undergrowth. This ambient noise is so constant and so deeply embedded in the experience of being in the bush that its absence is profoundly unsettling. And yet, witness after witness in the Blue Mountains has described a sudden, total cessation of all natural sound immediately before or during a Yowie encounter. The birds stop calling. The insects go quiet. The forest, in the space of a heartbeat, becomes absolutely still.

This phenomenon: sometimes called the "Oz Factor" by Australian researchers, though the term is used loosely and carries connotations this book does not endorse, deserves a more prosaic and more scientifically grounded explanation than it typically receives. What witnesses are describing is a localized ecological response to the presence of a large, unfamiliar organism. It is the same response observed when any apex-level disturbance enters an ecosystem: prey species go silent to avoid detection. It has been documented in the presence of large pythons, crocodiles, and raptors in Australian environments. It is the forest holding its breath; not a mystical event but a survival behavior, and its consistency in Yowie reports is evidence not of the supernatural but of something that the rest of the forest recognizes as significant.

Modern sighting reports from the Blue Mountains describe encounters on hiking trails, in campgrounds, near rural properties, and on the edges of small towns. The creature described is consistent with the broader Yowie profile; large, stocky, covered in dark hair, with a flat face and powerful build, but the Blue Mountains accounts often include a level of detail that comes from the relative proximity of the encounters. Witnesses have described the texture of the creature's hair, the smell of its body, the sound of its breathing, and the expression on its face. Several accounts describe the creature crouching or partially concealed behind vegetation, watching the witness with an unnerving stillness before either withdrawing or making an aggressive display. The Blue Mountains, for all their proximity to civilization, remain a landscape of deep gorges, cliff faces, and dense forest that has never been fully surveyed. The Grose Valley, the Colo River wilderness, the Wollemi National Park to the north; these are areas of genuine remoteness, where vertical sandstone cliffs create natural barriers and where the forest floor has been walked by few humans in recorded history. If the Yowie is a flesh-and-blood creature; a surviving population of some unknown species adapted to the Australian environment, then the Blue Mountains represent exactly the kind of terrain in which such a population could persist: close enough to human habitation to produce regular encounters, but rugged and vast enough to provide the deep refuge that a large, intelligent, and deliberately elusive creature would require.

Case Study: The 1977 Blue Mountains Confrontation
In 1977, a series of encounters reported near Springwood in the Blue Mountains drew regional media attention and renewed long-standing discussions of Yowie activity in the area. One report, frequently cited in later compilations, involved a pair of bushwalkers navigating a remote trail shortly before dusk.
The men reported hearing heavy movement paralleling their position approximately thirty meters inside dense scrub. Assuming it to be a kangaroo or wild pig, they continued walking until the sound abruptly stopped.
Then the bush went silent.
Bird activity ceased. Insect noise vanished. One of the men later stated that the air felt "pressurized," as though before a storm.
Moments later, a large figure emerged from behind a sandstone outcrop. It was described as approximately seven feet tall, extremely broad through the shoulders, and covered in dark, matted hair. The face was flat, with deep-set eyes that reflected red in the fading light. The men reported a strong, musky odor similar to wet animal hide. The creature did not retreat. It took several steps toward them, vocalizing in a low, guttural growl before releasing a higher, shrieking sound. One witness raised his arms and shouted in response. The

creature reportedly struck a nearby tree trunk with force before turning and disappearing downslope into heavy vegetation.

No physical injury occurred. No pursuit followed. The encounter lasted less than thirty seconds.

What differentiates this case from casual sightings is the close-range interaction and the performative aggression. The behavior mirrored documented primate threat displays; loud, physical, designed to intimidate rather than attack. The smell, the eye shine, the silence that preceded the encounter, the vocalization, and the aggressive display followed by withdrawal; every element is consistent with the broader Yowie pattern and with primate ethology generally.

As with so many Yowie reports, the confrontation ended not in violence but in mutual withdrawal. The creature enforced its boundary. The humans respected it. The forest resumed its noise. And the encounter became another entry in a record that, year by year, continues to grow.

Case Study: The Pilliga Nocturnal (2001)

Not all Yowie encounters fit the Blue Mountains template of confrontation and display. A report from the Pilliga Forest in northwestern New South Wales; one of the largest remaining areas of semi-arid woodland on the continent, illustrates a different behavioral mode.

In 2001, a pair of forestry workers conducting a nighttime fauna survey in the Pilliga reported observing a large, dark figure crossing a fire trail approximately fifty meters ahead of their vehicle. The figure was upright, moved with a fluid, unhurried gait, and was visible in the headlights for approximately four to five seconds before disappearing into the timber on the far side of the trail. The workers described it as approximately six feet tall, heavily built, and covered in dark hair. No sound was heard. No smell was detected at the distance involved. The creature did not acknowledge the vehicle or its occupants.

What makes this account noteworthy is its banality. There was no confrontation, no display, no dramatic encounter. The creature was simply moving through its environment, crossing an open space to reach cover, in the manner of any large animal navigating a fragmented landscape. The workers, both experienced in night survey work and familiar with the full range of Pilliga fauna; kangaroos, emus, feral pigs, foxes, stated that the figure did not match any known species and that its upright, bipedal gait was unlike anything they had previously observed.

The Pilliga account is important because it demonstrates that the Yowie behavioral repertoire is not limited to aggression and confrontation. In a habitat where human density is extremely low and encounters are rare; the creature's behavior appears to default to avoidance; the same pattern seen in the majority of Bigfoot reports from low-density wilderness. The confrontational behavior so characteristic of the Blue Mountains may be a response to compressed habitat and frequent human proximity rather than an inherent behavioral trait. If so, the Yowie's temperamental difference from Bigfoot may be less a matter of species character and more a matter of ecological circumstance; a hypothesis the comparative chapters will test.

The Continent That Shouldn't Have One

The Yowie is, in many respects, the most challenging cryptid examined in this volume. It lacks the fossil lineage that gives the Mapinguari its scientific plausibility. It lacks the sheer volume of physical evidence that characterizes the Bigfoot case. It exists on a continent whose evolutionary history offers no obvious explanation for its presence.

And yet the reports persist. The Aboriginal traditions: the oldest continuous body of oral testimony on Earth, describe it. The colonial records document it. The modern witnesses, many of them experienced bush professionals with no interest in publicity, continue to report it. The behavioral patterns are internally consistent and ethologically coherent. The geographic distribution follows the contours of habitat rather than the contours of culture or media influence.

The Yowie sits at the outer edge of plausibility, and it is aware, if we may speak metaphorically, that it does not belong. Everything about Australia's biology says that a large, bipedal, primate-like creature should not be there. And everything about the testimony says that something is.

In the chapters that follow, these three creatures; the Sasquatch of the deep timber, the Mapinguari of the twilight forest, and the Yowie of the sandstone gorges, will be placed side by side. Their similarities will be mapped. Their differences will be interrogated. The evidence for each will be weighed against the evidence for the others, and the patterns that emerge from that comparison will be followed wherever they lead.

The empty spaces on the map are not all the same shape. But they may share the same shadow.

Chapter 4: The Shared DNA: Similarities

The Same Silhouette

When one steps back from the individual accounts; from the Pacific Northwest timber to the Amazonian canopy to the Australian bush, and examines the three subjects side by side, what emerges is a silhouette. It is the same silhouette. Across three continents, three vastly different climates, and three entirely unrelated cultural traditions, witnesses have described, with a consistency that demands attention, a creature that conforms to a single basic template: a large, upright, bipedal figure, covered in hair, with a body plan that falls somewhere between that of a human being and that of a great ape.

This is not a trivial observation. The world is full of mythical creatures, and they come in an almost infinite variety of forms; dragons, sea serpents, winged beings, shapeshifters, entities with no fixed physical form at all. The human imagination, when left to its own devices, is extraordinarily creative. And yet, when the indigenous cultures of North America, South America, and Australia; cultures separated by oceans, millennia, and fundamental differences in language, cosmology, and daily life, independently generated their accounts of large, unknown creatures in the wilderness, they converged on the same form. Not a four-legged beast. Not a serpent or a bird. A biped. An upright walker. An ape-man.

The question this chapter must answer is how deep that convergence goes. If the similarities are confined to the broad outline; "big, hairy, walks on two legs", then the psychological explanation is probably sufficient. Humans fear the almost-human. The uncanny valley runs deep. A shared cognitive template could produce the same basic form across cultures without requiring a shared biological reality behind it. But if the similarities extend into the specific, the anatomical, the behavioral, and the ecological; if the three creatures share details that would be present in a real animal and absent from a psychological projection, then the convergence begins to point somewhere more interesting.

The evidence presented in the preceding three chapters suggests that the similarities are, in fact, far more specific than the broad outline alone. They penetrate into territory where the psychological explanation struggles and the biological one gains traction. This chapter maps that territory.

The Body Plan: More Than a Silhouette

The bipedal gait is the anchor of the convergence. All three creatures walk on two legs. This is described not as an occasional behavior; not the brief, opportunistic rearing-up that bears and other quadrupeds sometimes exhibit, but as the creature's primary mode of locomotion. Bigfoot walks. The Mapinguari walks, though it is also reported as capable of quadrupedal movement. The Yowie walks. They walk with a fluidity and confidence that witnesses consistently distinguish from the awkward bipedalism of known animals. The stride is long. The movement is purposeful. The body is balanced and centered in a way that implies a skeletal and muscular system specifically adapted for upright walking.

But bipedalism is only the beginning. When the physical descriptions are laid side by side in detail, a more specific composite emerges; one whose internal consistency is difficult to account for through independent invention.

The shoulders, across all three traditions, are described as enormously broad relative to the body. This is not a feature that generic "monster" descriptions tend to emphasize. Shoulders are not the stuff of nightmares. And yet witnesses on three continents independently report the same disproportionate breadth, often noting that the creature's shoulders are the single most striking feature of its silhouette. In Bigfoot accounts, the shoulders are frequently described as being half again as wide as a large man's. In Yowie reports, the torso is described as barrel-shaped, with a width through the chest that exceeds any human frame. In Mapinguari accounts, the creature's upper body is described as massively thick. The convergence on this specific proportion; not just "big" but specifically broad through the shoulders, is a detail that a shared psychological template does not obviously predict.

The arms present a similar pattern. All three creatures are described as having arms that are long relative to the torso, hanging to or past the knees. In Bigfoot accounts, this has been quantified through analysis of the Patterson-Gimlin film, where the arm-to-torso ratio falls outside the range of human anatomy. In Yowie accounts, the long arms are noted in conjunction with the creature's stocky build, creating an impression of a body designed for power rather than speed. In Mapinguari descriptions, the long, powerful arms are associated with large, curved claws; a detail that diverges from the other two but that is consistent with the ground sloth hypothesis specific to that creature. The neck, or rather, the absence of a visible neck, is another convergent detail. Across all three traditions, the head appears to sit directly on the shoulders, with no discernible neck separating the two. This is anatomically significant. In the great apes, the reduction of neck length is associated with the development of a sagittal crest; the bony ridge atop the skull that serves as an anchor for massive jaw muscles. In Bigfoot accounts, the conical or peaked skull shape has been explicitly linked to this feature. In Yowie accounts, the head is described as sitting "low on the shoulders" with a pronounced brow ridge. In Mapinguari accounts, detailed skull descriptions are rarer, but the overall impression of a head emerging directly from the torso is consistent.

The hair covering is universal but varies in ways that track with local ecology; a pattern that will be examined more closely in the next chapter on differences. For the purposes of this chapter, what matters is the convergence: all three creatures are described as covered in hair or fur over the entire body, with the face being the primary or only area of exposed skin. The hair is consistently described as coarse, thick, and somewhat matted; not the fine, groomed appearance of a well-kept animal, but the rough, weathered look of a creature that lives in the wild without any equivalent of grooming behavior.

The face, where described, presents the most variation of any feature; yet even here, the core architecture is consistent. All three creatures are described as having a broad, somewhat flat face with a heavy brow ridge, deep-set eyes, a wide nose, and a wide mouth. The overall arrangement is humanlike enough to be deeply unsettling but different enough to be immediately recognized as non-human. The flattened facial profile: the absence of a pronounced snout or muzzle, is a specifically primate feature, and its independent appearance across three traditions is one of the more quietly significant convergences in the data.

The Sensory Calling Cards

Beyond the visual similarities, there is a remarkable convergence in the sensory details associated with encounters across all three continents. These are not the broad strokes of physical description but the finer textures; the smells, the sounds, the peripheral phenomena that witnesses report alongside the visual sighting itself. And it is in these finer textures that the convergence becomes most difficult to explain away.

The Smell Gradient

The most consistent sensory detail across all three creatures is the smell. In North America, Bigfoot encounters are frequently accompanied by a powerful, unpleasant odor variously described as resembling rotten eggs, sulfur, wet dog, or the musk of an extremely large animal. In the Amazon, the Mapinguari's stench is one of its defining characteristics; a smell so overwhelming that it precedes the creature itself and is reported as causing nausea and temporary incapacitation. In Australia, Yowie encounters are associated with a strong, foul odor most often compared to wet animal hide or ammonia, though the descriptions are generally less extreme than those from either North America or the Amazon.

What emerges from the three-way comparison is not a single, uniform odor but a gradient; from the Mapinguari's incapacitating stench at one extreme, through Bigfoot's powerful musk in the middle, to the Yowie's strong but somewhat less overwhelming scent at the other end. This gradient is interesting because it does not follow the pattern that a culturally transmitted myth would predict. If the smell were a narrative embellishment; a storytelling device added for dramatic effect, we would expect it to appear with roughly equal intensity across all three traditions, or to be most extreme in the tradition with the greatest appetite for dramatic storytelling. Instead, the intensity of the reported odor correlates with a specific ecological variable: the density and visibility of the habitat.

The Mapinguari, which produces the most extreme odor, inhabits the Amazon; an environment where visibility is often limited to a few dozen yards and where chemical signaling would be the most effective means of long-distance territorial communication. Bigfoot, with a strong but less incapacitating odor, inhabits forests that are dense but generally more open than the Amazon understory. The Yowie, with the least extreme odor of the three, inhabits habitats that range from dense rainforest to relatively open eucalyptus woodland; environments where visual signaling is more feasible and chemical signaling correspondingly less critical.

If these creatures are real animals, the smell gradient maps precisely onto what a comparative biologist would predict: chemical communication intensity scaling with habitat density. If they are psychological projections, the gradient is an extraordinary coincidence; a detail that no storyteller had any reason to calibrate to local ecology, appearing calibrated, nonetheless.

The Soundscape

Country Cousins: Bigfoot, Mapinguari and the Yowie

The auditory dimension presents a similar pattern of convergence. Across all three regions, witnesses report hearing unusual vocalizations in association with encounters: deep howls, screams, whoops, sustained bellowing, and guttural calls that do not match known wildlife. The vocalizations share a common characteristic: they are low-frequency dominant, with a depth and resonance that implies a large chest cavity and a vocal apparatus of considerable power. Witnesses across all three traditions describe the same involuntary fear response; a gut-level dread that feels less like a reaction to a surprising noise and more like a physiological alarm triggered by something the nervous system recognizes as dangerous before the conscious mind has finished processing the sound.

But there is a more specific auditory phenomenon that connects the three cases in a way that pure vocalizations do not: percussive communication.

In North America, wood knocking; the deliberate, rhythmic striking of wood against wood, is one of the most commonly reported auditory features of Bigfoot encounters and has been the subject of dedicated field research for decades. In Australia, Yowie encounters include reports of heavy percussive impacts on trees during threat displays, with the creature reportedly striking trunks with its fists or with objects. In the Amazon, the Mapinguari's approach is sometimes preceded by rhythmic, heavy footfalls described as having a deliberate, almost ritualistic cadence; a percussive announcement that, while produced differently, serves the same apparent function: signaling presence across distance without requiring vocalization.

Wood knocking as a communicative behavior has a direct precedent in the animal kingdom. Chimpanzees engage in buttress drumming, striking the large root buttresses of tropical trees with their hands and feet to produce resonant, long-distance sounds that announce their presence, maintain group cohesion, and demarcate territory. The behavior is not random; it is structured, context-dependent, and socially meaningful. If the hairy humanoids of global tradition are, in fact, some form of primate or primate-like animal, the use of percussive communication would be not only plausible but expected; a strategy optimized for dense forest environments where visual signals fail and even vocal calls are attenuated by vegetation.

The convergence of percussive behavior across three independent traditions, in three different forest types, is one of the more quietly powerful similarities in the data. It is not a feature of generic monster mythology. No dragon knocks on trees. No sea serpent drums on logs. It is a specific, functional, ecologically grounded behavior that appears where a zoological hypothesis would predict it and where a psychological hypothesis has no obvious reason to place it.

Behavioral Convergence: The Way They Act

The physical and sensory convergences are striking, but it is in the behavioral patterns that the three-way comparison yields its most revealing results. Because behavior is where the specific and the functional intersect; where a creature's relationship to its environment is expressed in real time, and behavioral convergence across independent traditions is extraordinarily difficult to attribute to shared mythology.

The Universal Bluff

The single most important behavioral convergence across all three creatures is this: none of them has a confirmed record of killing a human being.

This statement requires a moment of reflection, because its implications are significant. All three creatures are described as large, powerful, and capable of causing serious physical harm. All three are described as engaging in intimidation behaviors; charging, vocalizing, throwing objects, striking trees. All three are reported from encounters in which the witness was alone, vulnerable, and in a location where help was unavailable. The conditions for lethal violence are, in many of these encounters, entirely present. And yet the violence does not occur. The charge stops short. The display ends. The creature withdraws.

This pattern: extreme intimidation without lethal follow-through, is the behavioral signature of a specific survival strategy, and it is one of the hallmarks of great ape ethology. Gorillas, chimpanzees, and orangutans all engage in dramatic threat displays that are, by design, disproportionate to their actual intent to harm. The display is the weapon. The physical confrontation it threatens is a last resort that the animal actively works to avoid, because physical combat carries injury risk for both parties. This cost-benefit calculation is not instinctive in the simple sense; it requires a degree of behavioral flexibility and situational awareness that is associated with higher cognitive function.

All three creatures appear to operate according to this principle. Bigfoot's behavioral repertoire: paralleling, wood knocking, bluff charging, rock throwing, represents a graduated escalation ladder designed to drive intruders away without physical engagement. The Mapinguari's territorial display; the stench, the roar, the advance-and-hold, serves the same function through different sensory channels. The Yowie's confrontational approach: the growling, the tree-striking, the aggressive lunges, is the most overtly frightening of the three but still terminates in withdrawal rather than attack.

The convergence here is not on a single behavior but on a behavioral strategy; a system of graduated deterrence that prioritizes territorial enforcement over physical confrontation. This is far more specific than "the creature is aggressive," which a shared mythology could easily produce. It is a calibrated, context-sensitive behavioral framework that mirrors the ethology of known great apes. Either three independent cultures invented the same sophisticated behavioral ecology, or they are observing the same type of animal.

Habitat Avoidance and the Encounter Gradient

A second behavioral convergence concerns the creatures' relationship to human presence. All three are described as primarily avoidant;

preferring to remain unseen and making contact only when human activity intrudes into their core territory. But the degree of avoidance varies in a pattern that tracks with habitat density and human population pressure; a pattern that the individual chapters flagged and that the comparison brings into sharp focus.

Bigfoot, operating in the vast, low-density wilderness of the Pacific Northwest and continental North America, is the most avoidant. Encounters are typically brief, distant, and initiated by the creature's accidental detection rather than by deliberate approach. The behavioral default is withdrawal.

The Mapinguari, in the deep Amazon, occupies an intermediate position. Encounters are rare but intense; the creature does not flee silently but announces its presence with overwhelming sensory force before withdrawing. The behavioral default is warning.

The Yowie, in the more compressed, fragmented habitat of the Australian eastern ranges, is the most confrontational. Encounters are closer, more prolonged, and more likely to involve direct approach by the creature. The behavioral default is assertion.

This gradient: avoidance in expansive habitat, warning in remote but finite habitat, confrontation in compressed habitat, is exactly the pattern that behavioral ecology would predict for a territorial species under varying degrees of spatial pressure. An animal with abundant territory and minimal human contact can afford to avoid. An animal with adequate territory but occasional intrusion escalates to warning. An animal whose territory is increasingly encroached upon escalates further to active deterrence.

The fact that three independent traditions describe a behavioral gradient that correlates with habitat pressure, without any mechanism for the witnesses to have coordinated their accounts, is among the most compelling convergences in this entire analysis.

The Watchers

There is one behavioral detail that appears across all three traditions with a specificity that deserves particular attention: the act of watching.

Bigfoot witnesses frequently describe the sensation of being observed before the creature is visually detected; a feeling of focused attention from the forest that precedes any visual or auditory confirmation. In North America, the behavior of paralleling, moving through the forest on a course parallel to a human traveler, maintaining distance and matching pace; is one of the most commonly reported behavioral patterns. The Yowie is described as watching witnesses through windows, from behind vegetation, and from concealed positions with an unnerving stillness that suggests sustained, deliberate observation. The Mapinguari, while less commonly described as a watcher in the visual sense, is reported as maintaining awareness of human presence across a wide territorial range; the smell and the roar function as evidence of a creature that has already detected the intruder before the intruder detects it.

In all three cases, the creature is described as the observer rather than the observed. The human is the one being watched, evaluated, and responded to. The encounters are not random collisions between a human and an animal that happens to be in the same space. They are interactions initiated by a creature that has been aware of the human presence for some time and has made a decision about how to respond. This reversal of the observer-observed relationship is deeply characteristic of encounters with intelligent, socially complex animals. Field primatologists working with habituated chimpanzee and gorilla groups describe the same experience; the awareness that the animal has been watching them long before they were aware of the animal. It implies a level of environmental awareness, attentional control, and decision-making capacity that goes well beyond the behavioral range of non-primate mammals.

The Nocturnal Convergence

All three creatures are reported as primarily crepuscular or nocturnal. Bigfoot encounters concentrate in the hours between dusk and dawn. The Mapinguari is most often encountered during the transitional hours of twilight or in conditions of deep forest shade. The Yowie shows the most pronounced nocturnal pattern of the three, with the majority of close-range encounters occurring after dark.

The convergence on nocturnal activity is significant for two reasons. First, it is ecologically coherent. Large-bodied animals in forest environments face thermoregulatory challenges during daylight hours, particularly in warm climates. Shifting primary activity to the cooler hours of darkness is a standard adaptation; employed by tapirs, jaguars, many ungulates, and numerous large marsupials. A large, hair-covered biped would face this pressure in all three habitats, and nocturnal activity would be the expected response.

Second, and more importantly, the nocturnal pattern provides a single, coherent explanation for what is otherwise the most damaging objection to all three creatures' existence: the absence of clear photographic evidence. The question "Why hasn't anyone gotten a clear photograph?" has haunted cryptid research since the invention of the portable camera. The answer, if the nocturnal data is taken seriously, is that the question is poorly framed. We do not have clear photographs of most nocturnal wildlife without the use of specialized equipment deployed in known locations with predictable animal movement patterns. A creature that is intelligent enough to avoid camera traps, active primarily during darkness, and operating in dense forest cover is not simply difficult to photograph. It is, by the intersection of those three factors, almost impossible to photograph; not because it does not exist, but because it has optimized, whether by instinct or intelligence, for invisibility during the hours when human visual technology is most effective.

This does not prove the creatures exist. But it demonstrates that the absence of photographic evidence is not the devastating argument against existence that it is commonly assumed to be. It is, rather, a predictable consequence of the behavioral and ecological profile that witnesses consistently describe.

The Witness Profile

There is one final convergence that operates not at the level of the creature but at the level of the person who encounters it, and it is worth examining because it speaks to the reliability of the source data that underlies everything else in this chapter.

Across all three traditions, the most detailed and credible encounter reports come from a consistent type of witness: a working person with extensive experience in the relevant wilderness environment, no prior interest in cryptids or the paranormal, and significant social and professional incentive to remain silent about their experience.

In North America, the core witness population for Bigfoot encounters consists of loggers, hunters, forestry workers, and rural residents; people who spend their working lives in the forest and who can identify every known animal in their territory by sight, sound, and track. In the Amazon, the most compelling Mapinguari testimony comes from the *seringueiros*, rubber tappers who spent months alone in deep forest, and from indigenous hunters with lifelong expertise in their local fauna. In Australia, the most detailed Yowie reports come from bushwalkers, forestry workers, and rural property owners with decades of experience in the Australian bush.

These witness populations share several characteristics that bear directly on the credibility of their testimony. They are experienced in their environments to a degree that makes simple misidentification unlikely. They have no cultural or personal investment in the existence of the creature; many had never heard of it before their encounter. They have strong social and professional incentives not to report what they saw, and many only do so years later, reluctantly, and often under conditions of anonymity. The emotional register of their accounts is consistent across continents: confusion, fear, reluctance to speak, and a persistent conviction that what they saw was real, paired with an awareness that saying so publicly will damage their credibility.

The convergence of witness profile is not proof of anything. But it is a pattern that any evaluation of the evidence must account for. If the phenomenon is purely psychological; if these creatures exist only in the minds of their observers, then the psychological explanation must account for the fact that the people most susceptible to the experience are, consistently, those with the most expertise in distinguishing real animals from imagined ones.

The Liminal Dwellers

There is one final similarity that transcends the physical and enters the realm of the conceptual, and it may be the most important of all. Bigfoot, the Mapinguari, and the Yowie do not inhabit the centers of things. They do not live in the open. They are not found in the places where human civilization is firmly established and the landscape is fully known. They exist at the edges.

In North America, Bigfoot is a creature of the deep timber; the old-growth forests, the mountain ridges, the wilderness areas where logging roads peter out and GPS signals fade. In the Amazon, the Mapinguari haunts the regions furthest from human settlement, the places where even indigenous communities acknowledge that the forest is no longer theirs. In Australia, the Yowie inhabits the gorges, the ranges, and the dense bush at the boundary between the settled coastal strip and the vast, unknowable interior.

These are liminal spaces, thresholds between the known and the unknown, the mapped and the unmapped, the human and the wild. And the creatures that inhabit them are, in every cultural tradition, liminal beings. They are not fully animal and not fully human. They are not entirely physical and not entirely spiritual. They exist in a space that defies clean categorization, and they seem to define, by their very presence, the boundary beyond which human authority does not extend.

But the liminal quality is not merely symbolic. It has an ecological dimension that is worth stating plainly: the edges of the known world are, by definition, the places where unknown things are most likely to be found. The deep forests, the remote gorges, the interior reaches of the largest wilderness areas on Earth; these are the habitats least surveyed, least monitored, and least understood by modern science. If a large, intelligent, deliberately elusive animal were to survive undetected into the twenty-first century, these are precisely the habitats in which it would do so. The liminality of these creatures is not only a mythological motif. It is an ecological prediction.

And the creatures' consistent positioning at the boundary between human and wild space is itself a behavioral choice; one that implies an awareness of where that boundary lies and a deliberate strategy of remaining on the far side of it. An animal that is merely reclusive would be distributed randomly with respect to human settlement. An animal that is specifically boundary-aware would concentrate at the edge, close enough to occasionally encounter humans, far enough to avoid sustained contact. This is, in fact, exactly the distribution pattern that all three creatures exhibit.

Whether this boundary-awareness reflects simple habitat preference, learned avoidance, or something more cognitively sophisticated is a question the evidence cannot yet answer. But the pattern is real, it is consistent across three continents, and it is the kind of detail that separates a living animal from a campfire story.

The Absence at the Center

There is one more convergence; the most uncomfortable one, that must be named before this chapter closes. It is the convergence of absence. None of these creatures has produced a type specimen. No body has been recovered. No bones have been found. No tissue sample has been submitted to a laboratory and confirmed as belonging to an unknown species. Across three continents, thousands of reported encounters, and more than a century of active investigation, the single most important piece of evidence; the one that would resolve the question definitively, has not materialized.

This absence is not a minor detail. It is the central fact of the entire phenomenon, and it applies with equal force to all three creatures. The Bigfoot case has the deepest evidence base; thousands of track casts, the Patterson-Gimlin film, the Sierra Sounds, the Skookum Cast, and yet no body. The Mapinguari case has the most plausible fossil lineage and the most biologically compelling habitat, and yet no body. The Yowie case has the oldest continuous oral tradition on Earth supporting it, and yet no body.

The shared absence of definitive proof is, in one reading, the strongest argument against the existence of all three creatures. If they are real, where are the remains? Animals die. Bones persist. In an age of environmental DNA, satellite imagery, and camera trap networks, how can a large-bodied animal on three continents evade confirmation? These are fair questions, and they will receive their full treatment in the chapters that follow. For now, it is enough to note that the absence is itself a convergence; one that is either the signature of a shared non-existence or the signature of a shared biological strategy of evasion so effective that it has, so far, outpaced our capacity to overcome it. The comparative method cannot resolve this question on its own. But by establishing how deep the other convergences run; how specific, how consistent, how ecologically calibrated the similarities between these three creatures are; it can determine how much weight the absence should carry.

If the similarities were shallow; if the three creatures shared nothing but a vague silhouette and a habit of being seen in forests, then the absence of proof would be dispositive. There would be nothing left to explain.

But the similarities are not shallow. They are deep, specific, and patterned in ways that track with ecology rather than mythology. The smell gradient follows habitat density. The behavioral gradient follows spatial pressure. The anatomical details converge on features that serve functional rather than narrative purposes. The witness populations share a profile that is the opposite of what a hoax or a mass delusion would predict.

The shared silhouette is not just a silhouette. It is a blueprint, and whether the building it describes stands in the forest or only in the human mind is the question that the rest of this book will pursue.

Comparative Profile — Volume I

Feature	Bigfoot (N. America)	Mapinguari (Amazon)	Yowie (Australia)
Average Reported Height	7–10 ft	6–8 ft	5–8 ft
Build	Tall, broad-shouldered	Massive, thick-torsoed	Stocky, compact, powerful
Primary Habitat	Temperate/boreal forest	Deep *terra firme* rainforest	Mountain bush, gorges, wet sclerophyll
Climate Adaptation	Cold-adapted, large body mass	Dense fur, humidity tolerance, osteoderms	Compact build, heat/drought resilience
Locomotion	Bipedal (primary)	Bipedal and quadrupedal	Bipedal (primary)
Foot Morphology	Mid-tarsal break, flexible arch	Unusual tracks, possible reversed appearance	Large, flat, rigid profile

Feature	Bigfoot (N. America)	Mapinguari (Amazon)	Yowie (Australia)
Odor Intensity	Strong (musky, sulfuric)	Extreme (incapacitating, putrid)	Moderate–strong (musky, animal)
Vocalizations	Howls, screams, whoops	Deep sustained roar/bellow	Growls, shrieks, guttural calls
Percussive Communication	Wood knocking (well documented)	Rhythmic footfalls, possible tree strikes	Tree strikes during displays
Aggression Pattern	Avoidant / graduated deterrence	Territorial warning / stand-off	Confrontational display / bluff charge
Nocturnal Activity	Strong (majority of close encounters)	Moderate–strong (crepuscular/low-light)	Pronounced (majority after dark)
Eye Shine	Reported (reddish-orange, amber)	Rarely described	Frequently reported (red)
Lethal Attacks on Humans	None confirmed	None confirmed	None confirmed
Core Witness Population	Loggers, hunters, rural residents	*Seringueiros*, indigenous hunters	Bushwalkers, forestry workers
Physical Evidence Depth	Extensive (tracks, film, audio, casts)	Sparse (tracks, hair, scat)	Thin (tracks, hair)

Feature	Bigfoot (N. America)	Mapinguari (Amazon)	Yowie (Australia)
Biological Hypothesis	Relict hominoid / *Gigantopithecus*	Surviving ground sloth descendant	Unknown (primate crossing? convergent marsupial?)
Fossil Lineage Support	Moderate (*Gigantopithecus* in Asia)	Strong (ground sloths in S. America)	None (no primates in Australian record)
Indigenous Oral Tradition Depth	Thousands of years	Thousands of years	60,000+ years
Spiritual/Cultural Overlay	Moderate	High (transformed shaman, sacred enforcer)	Low–moderate (Dreamtime integration)
Habitat Threat Level	Moderate (logging, development)	Severe (deforestation, agriculture)	Moderate (fragmentation, fire)

Chapter 5: Evolutionary Divergence — Differences

The Environmental Adaptation

If the similarities between these three creatures suggest a common signal; a shared template operating across continents, then the differences suggest something equally important: that the signal, whatever its nature, has been shaped and reshaped by forces specific to each location. And these differences are not minor. They are deep, structural, and profoundly responsive to the landscapes in which each creature is said to dwell.

The previous chapter established that the convergences between Bigfoot, the Mapinguari, and the Yowie are too specific and too ecologically calibrated to be comfortably dismissed as shared mythology. This chapter asks the complementary question: are the divergences equally calibrated? Do the differences between the three creatures track with the differences between their environments in the way that biological adaptation would predict? Or are they random, arbitrary, distributed in patterns that suggest cultural invention rather than ecological response?

The answer, as with the similarities, is more complicated and more interesting than either extreme. Some differences map onto ecology with striking precision. Others resist biological explanation entirely and point toward the cultural, the psychological, or the genuinely anomalous. Mapping that distinction; sorting the ecologically coherent from the biologically inexplicable, is the work of this chapter.

The Thermal Gradient: Bodies Shaped by Climate

The most immediately apparent physical differences between the three creatures follow a pattern that any biologist would recognize: they track with temperature.

The Bigfoot of North America is, in its most essential physical characteristics, a creature of the cold. The Pacific Northwest, the Northern Rockies, the boreal forests of Canada; these are environments defined by harsh winters, heavy snowfall, and temperatures that plunge well below freezing for months at a time. The Bigfoot described by witnesses is physically suited to these conditions. The thick, often dark-colored hair covering its body functions as insulation; a dense, full-body coat analogous to the fur of a bear or a mountain goat, designed to retain heat and shed water. The creature's immense size is itself an adaptation. Bergmann's Rule, one of the foundational principles of ecogeography, states that within a species or group of closely related species, individuals in colder climates tend to be larger than those in warmer environments, because a larger body has a lower surface-area-to-volume ratio and therefore loses heat more slowly. The Bigfoot's reported seven-to-ten-foot stature fits this principle precisely.

The inverse of Bergmann's Rule; that individuals in warmer climates should be smaller, predicts the size gradient that the data actually shows. The Mapinguari of the Amazon, inhabiting the hottest and most humid of the three environments, is reported at six to eight feet: shorter than Bigfoot by a meaningful margin. The Yowie of Australia, facing not tropical heat but the extreme temperature variability of a continent where summer days can exceed 115 degrees Fahrenheit and winter nights in the mountains drop below freezing, is reported at five to eight feet; the shortest and most compact of the three, with a build that emphasizes breadth and muscle mass over height.

This size gradient: tallest in the coldest habitat, shortest in the most thermally variable, is not the pattern that cultural invention would produce. If these creatures were independent mythological constructions, there would be no reason for their reported sizes to correlate with the thermal environments in which they are placed. A culture inventing a monster has every reason to make it as large as possible; size is frightening, size is dramatic, size sells stories. The fact that the reported sizes instead follow the precise ecological principle that governs body size in real mammals is either a coincidence of unusual specificity or evidence that something real is being described.

But the thermal gradient extends beyond size. The quality and function of the body covering differs across the three in ways that are ecologically coherent.

Bigfoot's fur is most commonly described as thick, full, and relatively uniform; the insulating coat of a cold-climate mammal. The Mapinguari's fur is described as long, coarse, matted, and armor-like; a covering adapted not primarily for warmth but for physical protection against the thorns, biting insects, parasites, and constant abrasion of moving through dense tropical undergrowth. The embedded bony osteoderms hypothesized by those who link the creature to the giant ground sloths would represent the ultimate expression of this protective adaptation; a living suit of chainmail evolved under the specific pressures of the Amazon. The Yowie's hair covering is described as somewhat shorter and coarser than Bigfoot's, consistent with an animal in a warmer climate that retains enough covering for nighttime insulation and physical protection in rugged terrain but does not need the dense thermal layer required in the Pacific Northwest. Each covering solves a different problem. Bigfoot's solves cold. The Mapinguari's solves the rainforest's mechanical assault on skin. The Yowie's solves thermal variability. Three environments, three solutions; calibrated to local conditions with a specificity that, again, has no obvious mythological motivation.

The Feet Tell Different Stories

The foot morphology divergence across the three creatures is among the most technically significant differences in the comparative dataset, and it has received far less attention than it deserves.

Bigfoot footprints; the most extensively documented of the three, display the mid-tarsal break identified by Jeff Meldrum: a flexion point in the midfoot that produces a pressure ridge across the center of the print. This feature suggests a foot adapted for bipedal locomotion on soft, uneven forest floor; a flexible foot that sacrifices the spring-loaded efficiency of the human arch for greater compliance on yielding surfaces. The foot is long; typically, sixteen to eighteen inches, with five distinct toes, visible toe splay, and in the best casts, dermal ridges analogous to fingerprints. It is, in its essential architecture, a primate foot; large and unusual but recognizably derived from the same lineage as the human foot.

The Mapinguari leaves tracks of a fundamentally different character. The prints described by researchers are large but do not display the five-toed, primate-like morphology of Bigfoot tracks. Instead, they show a rounded, somewhat elongated impression with apparent claw marks at the leading edge; a morphology far more consistent with the foot anatomy of a ground sloth than with any primate. Ground sloths walked on the outer edges and knuckles of their hind feet, with massive claws curling inward, producing tracks that would be immediately and profoundly unfamiliar to any human tracker. The backward-feet tradition; the persistent indigenous claim that the Mapinguari's feet point in the wrong direction, may be the cultural processing of exactly this unfamiliarity: tracks that do not follow the rules of any known animal, interpreted as tracks that face the wrong way.

The Yowie's footprints present yet a third morphology. Where documented, they are large; fourteen to eighteen inches, and broadly humanoid in shape, with five toes and a heel impression. But they lack the mid-tarsal break of Bigfoot prints, displaying instead a flatter, more rigid profile. The toe splay is wider than human norms, but the overall architecture is less flexible than the Bigfoot foot, suggesting a different locomotor adaptation; perhaps a foot suited to the hard, rocky terrain of the Australian ranges rather than the soft forest duff of the Pacific Northwest.

Three feet. Three morphologies. Three distinct solutions to three distinct locomotor challenges. This is precisely the pattern of divergent adaptation that evolutionary biology predicts when a common body plan is subjected to different selective pressures. And it is a pattern that would be extraordinarily difficult to produce through independent cultural invention, because feet are not the stuff of mythology. No storytelling tradition has reason to calibrate the biomechanics of its monster's foot to the substrate characteristics of the local terrain. The foot differences are invisible to narrative. They are visible only to analysis.

What They Eat, and What It Means

The dietary profiles proposed for the three creatures diverge as sharply as their habitats, and these divergences carry direct implications for the ecological feasibility analyses that later chapters will pursue.

Bigfoot is most plausibly modeled as a large-bodied omnivore; a dietary generalist exploiting the rich and seasonally variable food base of North American temperate and boreal forests. The proposed diet centers on high-calorie plant material (berries, roots, tubers, cambium) supplemented by opportunistic protein sources including fish during spawning runs, small mammals, and possibly deer. This dietary profile closely parallels that of the black bear, which occupies the same habitat, has a comparable body mass, and sustains itself on essentially the same food web. The seasonal correlation between Bigfoot sighting peaks and salmon runs in Pacific Northwest river systems supports this model. If Bigfoot exists, it eats like a bear; broadly, opportunistically, and in sync with the seasonal pulse of forest productivity.

The Mapinguari, if it is a surviving ground sloth descendant, would be primarily herbivorous. The isotopic record of known ground sloth species confirms a plant-based diet of leaves, bark, roots, and fruit, with powerful forelimbs and massive claws used to access food sources beyond the reach of smaller browsers. In the Amazon, this dietary strategy would orient the creature toward palms and their fruits, forest-floor tubers, the soft inner bark of certain tree species, and the fungal communities that proliferate in rotting wood. Several indigenous accounts describe the Mapinguari feeding on specific plants; a detail that, as noted in Chapter 2, carries the ecological specificity of real observation rather than the vagueness of invention.

A large herbivore in the Amazon would need to consume thirty to fifty pounds of plant material daily, but the forest provides this in abundance. The dietary constraint is not supply but detectability, whether an animal consuming that volume of vegetation would leave traces obvious enough to be found.

The Yowie faces the most challenging dietary environment of the three. Australia's dominant vegetation: eucalyptus, is effectively inedible to most mammals, its leaves saturated with toxic oils and offering minimal nutritional value. A large, active omnivore in the Australian eastern forests would need to exploit non-eucalyptus food sources: rainforest fruits where available, roots and tubers, freshwater crayfish and fish from the creek systems that thread through the gorge country, and critically; the substantial populations of marsupials, wallabies, and ground-nesting birds that share the habitat. The Yowie's dietary profile, to the extent that it can be reconstructed, resembles not a primate's diet but a bear's; and Australia, notably, has no bears. The Yowie, if real, may occupy an ecological niche that has been vacant on the continent since the megafaunal extinctions forty-six thousand years ago.

The dietary divergence is significant for several reasons. It means that the three creatures, if real, are not simply the same animal in different locations. They are three different ecological entities; an omnivore, an herbivore, and a predator-omnivore, that share a body plan but occupy fundamentally different positions in their respective food webs. This has direct implications for population modeling: an herbivore in the Amazon requires a different home range, produces different trace evidence, and faces different reproductive constraints than an omnivore in the Pacific Northwest or a predator-omnivore in Australia. The ecological feasibility of each creature must be assessed independently, on terms specific to its habitat and diet; a point that the relevant later chapter will develop in detail.

Three Lineages, or None

The fossil lineage question is where the three cases diverge most dramatically, and where the comparative method encounters its most uncomfortable tension.

The Bigfoot case has a candidate ancestor: *Gigantopithecus blacki*, the enormous ape known from fossil teeth and jawbones recovered in China and Southeast Asia. *Gigantopithecus* lived from approximately nine million years ago to roughly three hundred thousand years ago, stood an estimated ten feet tall, and is the largest primate known to have existed. The geographic and temporal gap between *Gigantopithecus* in Asia and a hypothetical descendant in North America is substantial; it requires a crossing of Beringia during one of the Pleistocene glacial periods, but it is not physically impossible. Humans made the same crossing. So did bears, wolves, mammoths, and dozens of other species. A *Gigantopithecus* descendant crossing into North America and adapting to the temperate forests of the Pacific Northwest is speculative, but it fits within the known framework of Pleistocene biogeography.

The Mapinguari case has a stronger candidate lineage: the giant ground sloths of South America. Multiple genera: *Megatherium, Eremotherium, Mylodon*, are documented from the same geographic region where the Mapinguari is reported, and they were present until approximately eleven thousand years ago. The physical parallels between the Mapinguari descriptions and the known anatomy of ground sloths are specific and numerous: the size, the upright posture, the dense fur, the osteoderms, the large claws. The Mapinguari case does not need to posit a transoceanic crossing or an undocumented migration. It needs only to posit that a population of ground sloths; or a descendant species, survived the Pleistocene extinction in the deep Amazon, a habitat with the size, the remoteness, and the ecological buffering capacity to make such survival at least plausible.

The Yowie case has no candidate lineage at all. Australia's fossil record contains no primates; not a fragment, not a trace, across the entire span of the continent's post-Gondwanan isolation. This is not a gap that future discovery is likely to fill, because the Australian mammalian fossil record is well-sampled enough that the complete absence of primates is almost certainly real. The Yowie, if it is a biological entity, must have arrived through Pleistocene migration from Southeast Asia (as humans did) or must be something other than a primate entirely; perhaps a product of Australia's documented capacity for convergent evolution, a marsupial that independently evolved a primate-like body plan.

This divergence in fossil support creates an asymmetry in the three cases that the comparative method must acknowledge honestly. The Mapinguari has the strongest paleontological foundation. Bigfoot has a plausible but geographically strained one. The Yowie has none. If fossil lineage support were the only criterion, the Mapinguari would be the most credible of the three, the Yowie the least, and Bigfoot somewhere in between. But fossil lineage is not the only criterion; it is one variable among many, and the Yowie's weakness on this axis does not invalidate the strengths it shows on others. It does, however, mean that the Yowie case must work harder to explain itself, and any unified theory of the three creatures must be flexible enough to accommodate the possibility that they do not share a single evolutionary origin.

The Aggression Spectrum

Chapter 4 established that all three creatures share a behavioral strategy of graduated deterrence; escalating threat displays that stop short of lethal violence. This chapter must now examine the significant differences in how that strategy is expressed, because the variation is not random. It tracks with ecology.

Bigfoot is the most avoidant of the three. The creature's default behavioral mode is withdrawal; it detects human presence, it moves away, and the encounter ends with a glimpse or with indirect evidence (footprints, vocalizations, broken vegetation). When Bigfoot does engage in threat displays, they tend to be non-visual: wood knocking, rock throwing from concealment, vocalizations from a distance. The creature escalates reluctantly and retreats readily. Close-range confrontations are rare in the Bigfoot record, and when they occur, they are typically brief.

The Mapinguari occupies the middle of the spectrum. It does not retreat silently; it announces its presence with overwhelming sensory force. The stench, the roar, the heavy approach; these are assertive warnings delivered from a position of confidence. But the Mapinguari does not close distance in the way the Yowie does. Its defensive strategy is to make the environment intolerable; to fill the sensory space with signals so overwhelming that the intruder has no choice but to leave. The warning is the point. The creature holds its position or advances slowly; the intruder flees.

The Yowie is the most confrontational of the three. It approaches, closes distance, vocalizes at close range, strikes objects, and makes aggressive physical movements directly toward the witness. The Blue Mountains encounters and the broader Australian record are dominated by accounts of direct, face-to-face interactions at distances of twenty meters or less; ranges that would be extremely unusual in the Bigfoot literature and virtually unheard of in Mapinguari accounts.

This three-point gradient; avoidance, sensory deterrence, physical confrontation, correlates with a specific ecological variable: the spatial relationship between the creature and human populations.

Bigfoot operates in vast, low-density wilderness where retreat is almost always possible. A creature with thousands of square miles of forest can afford to avoid every encounter simply by moving away. The cost of avoidance is low, and the benefit, remaining undetected, is high.

The Mapinguari operates in remote but ecologically bounded habitat. The deep *terra firme* forests are vast, but they are bounded by river systems that create natural barriers. A creature whose territory is defined by river boundaries and forest edges cannot always retreat indefinitely; it must, at some point, stand its ground and deliver a deterrent signal powerful enough to turn the intruder back.

The Yowie operates in the most compressed habitat of the three. The Australian eastern ranges are, by comparison to the Pacific Northwest or the Amazon interior, geographically narrow; a strip of rugged country between the heavily settled coastal plain and the arid interior. A creature in this habitat faces more frequent human encounters at closer range, with fewer options for retreat. Under these conditions, escalation to confrontational display is not a personality trait; it is a survival response to spatial pressure. The creature cannot always avoid; it must sometimes assert.

This ecological interpretation reframes the behavioral differences not as evidence that the three creatures have fundamentally different temperaments but as evidence that the same underlying behavioral system; graduated deterrence, produces different outputs depending on the spatial constraints of the environment. It is the same animal responding to different pressures, or at least the same behavioral template expressed through different ecological filters.

Voices in Different Registers

The vocalization differences across the three creatures are specific enough to warrant individual treatment, because they diverge not only in character but in apparent function.

Bigfoot's vocal repertoire is the most extensively documented, thanks to decades of field recording in North America. The range includes howls, screams, whoops, grunts, and the sustained "Primal Scream" that has been captured on spectrographic analysis. But the most extraordinary element; unique to Bigfoot among the three, is the apparent language captured in the Sierra Sounds. If R. Scott Nelson's cryptolinguistic analysis is even partially valid, Bigfoot may possess structured vocal communication: identifiable phonemes, repeated morphological units, and apparent syntax. No comparable claim has been made for either the Mapinguari or the Yowie.

This is a difference of enormous potential significance. If Bigfoot uses language and the other two creatures do not, it implies a level of cognitive complexity that separates Bigfoot from its counterparts by a wide margin: placing it closer to the human end of the cognitive spectrum than any known non-human primate. It would also represent a point of evidence in favor of the *Gigantopithecus* or hominid hypothesis for Bigfoot specifically, since the capacity for structured language is associated with brain structures found in the hominin lineage but not in other primates or in non-primate mammals.

The Mapinguari's vocal profile is simpler in structure but no less powerful in effect. The sustained, deep bellow; a resonant roar that witnesses describe as vibrating through the forest floor, is a single-note, high-volume territorial call optimized for transmission through dense tropical vegetation. It resembles the communication strategy of howler monkeys, which use low-frequency calls to broadcast territorial claims over miles of canopy. If the Mapinguari is a ground sloth descendant rather than a primate, a relatively simple vocal apparatus producing a powerful, low-frequency call would be more anatomically consistent than the complex vocalizations attributed to Bigfoot. Ground sloths were not primates and would not be expected to possess the laryngeal and neural architecture required for language-like vocalization.

The Yowie's vocalizations fall between the other two: more varied than the Mapinguari's single bellow but lacking the structural complexity attributed to Bigfoot's Sierra Sounds. The Australian reports describe growls, grunts, shrieks, and a distinctive high-pitched call that witnesses have been unable to compare to any known Australian wildlife. These are communicative but apparently non-linguistic, threat displays, alarm calls, and territorial assertions rather than structured information exchange. This vocal profile is consistent with that of a large, non-human primate or, if the convergent marsupial hypothesis is entertained, with a large mammal that has developed a moderately complex vocal repertoire without approaching linguistic capacity.

The vocalization gradient: from potentially linguistic (Bigfoot) through simple but powerful (Mapinguari) to moderately complex but non-linguistic (Yowie), may reflect the different evolutionary lineages hypothesized for each creature. A hominid-lineage Bigfoot might produce language. A ground sloth-lineage Mapinguari would not. A Yowie of uncertain lineage falls somewhere in between. The vocal data, insofar as it is reliable, does not contradict the lineage hypotheses proposed for each creature. It is consistent with them.

Cultural Lenses: Three Ways of Being Monsters

The physical differences between these three creatures are mirrored, and in some ways amplified, by the cultural lenses through which they are viewed. Each creature exists not only as a biological possibility in the testimony of its witnesses but as a cultural entity in the traditions of its homeland, and the meanings assigned to each reveal as much about the cultures as they do about the creatures themselves.

In North America, Bigfoot has been progressively domesticated by popular culture. While the indigenous traditions of the Sasquatch are rich, complex, and sometimes quite dark, the dominant cultural image of Bigfoot in the modern Western imagination is overwhelmingly that of the Gentle Giant; a shy, retiring woodland creature that wants nothing more than to be left alone. This characterization is reinforced by decades of popular media, from family-friendly documentaries to children's cartoons, and it reflects a broader cultural attitude toward the wilderness as a place of retreat and solace rather than danger. Bigfoot, in the American imagination, is what the wild has become: something diminished, something endangered, something more to be pitied than feared.

This cultural framing has consequences for the evidence. The Gentle Giant narrative encourages a certain type of witness behavior, approaching rather than fleeing, searching for tracks rather than reporting to authorities, interpreting ambiguous signals as signs of a benign presence rather than a threatening one. It shapes what gets reported and how, creating a feedback loop in which the cultural expectation and the evidence base reinforce each other.

The Mapinguari occupies an entirely different cultural space. In the Amazonian traditions, it is not gentle and it is not pitied. It is the Spirit Enforcer; a being of supernatural power, a guardian of the deep forest that punishes those who trespass too far into the wild. The cultural function of the Mapinguari is explicitly cautionary. It marks the boundary between the human world and the world of forces that do not answer to human authority. The transformation narrative: the shaman punished for his arrogance, places the Mapinguari squarely within a moral framework. It is not simply an animal to be avoided. It is a consequence to be feared.

This framing also has consequences for the evidence, though of a different kind. The Spirit Enforcer narrative discourages investigation. It frames the act of seeking the creature as itself a form of transgression; an arrogant violation of a boundary that exists for a reason. Indigenous communities that hold this view do not go looking for the Mapinguari. They do not set camera traps or collect hair samples. They respect the boundary that the creature represents. The result is that the Mapinguari operates within a cultural framework that actively protects it from systematic investigation; a protection that no amount of Western scientific interest has been able to fully overcome. The Yowie, true to its Australian character, is the Territorial Brute; neither gentle nor supernatural, but aggressive, physical, and immediate. The cultural framing of the Yowie reflects Australia's broader relationship with its landscape, which is less romantic than the North American model and less mystical than the Amazonian. The Australian bush is regarded with a pragmatic wariness born of hard experience. It is beautiful, but it is not safe. Things in the bush will hurt you, the snakes, the spiders, the heat, the distance, the isolation. The Yowie fits neatly into this framework as one more dangerous thing in a landscape full of dangerous things. It is to be respected, avoided, and survived, but it does not carry the spiritual freight of the Mapinguari or the cultural affection of Bigfoot.

These cultural interpretations are not mere decoration layered onto an underlying zoological reality. They are integral to the phenomenon. The way a culture understands and describes an encounter shapes the encounter itself; influencing what details are emphasized, what details are minimized, and what framework of meaning the witness uses to process an experience that, by definition, falls outside the boundaries of the ordinary. The Gentle Giant, the Spirit Enforcer, and the Territorial Brute may all describe the same basic biological template, shaped by local conditions into different forms. Or they may describe three very different things. What they unquestionably describe are three very different ways of being human in the wild, and three very different evidentiary landscapes, shaped as much by culture as by habitat.

The Physical Outliers

For all their similarities, the three creatures possess certain reported physical features that do not easily map onto one another and that resist incorporation into any single unified theory. These outliers are the rough edges of the comparative framework, and they deserve honest examination rather than quiet omission.

The Mapinguari's alleged single eye is one such feature. While not present in all accounts, the cyclopic description appears frequently enough in the testimony to constitute a genuine element of the tradition rather than an isolated embellishment. If taken as a literal physical characteristic, it places the Mapinguari outside the range of any known primate and, indeed, outside the range of any known large mammal. The single eye, however, may be a cultural interpretation of an unusual facial structure; a creature with a heavily ridged brow, deep-set eyes set close together, and a face covered in long hair might, in the limited visibility of the rainforest floor, appear to have a single eye when observed briefly and at a distance. Alternatively, the cyclopic motif may be entirely symbolic, carrying the same mythological weight it has borne in cultures around the world since the Greeks: the mark of the primitive, the inhuman, the one-who-sees-differently. The Mapinguari's second mouth; the abdominal opening described in certain accounts, stands as perhaps the most challenging physical outlier of all. No known mammal possesses such a feature, and no plausible biological mechanism fully explains it. Chapter 2 proposed three interpretations: the symbolic (a belly-mouth as universal marker of wrongness), the biological (a ventral scent gland misidentified under conditions of poor visibility and extreme fear), and the syncretic (a detail imported from the *Curupira* tradition and fused with the Mapinguari account over time). The second mouth may be the clearest example in this entire study of a detail that belongs to the spiritual rather than the zoological dimension of a tradition, and of the difficulty of separating the two when working with accounts that do not recognize the distinction.

The Yowie's glowing red eyes represent a different kind of outlier. While eyeshine is well-established zoology, the specific red coloration reported in Yowie encounters does not perfectly match the typical yellow, green, or amber eyeshine of most known Australian fauna. Red eyeshine can be produced under certain conditions of light angle and tapetum composition; several marsupial species produce reddish reflection under specific circumstances, but its consistent reporting in Yowie accounts suggests either a genuine physiological feature or a cultural expectation that has become embedded in the reporting template. Red or glowing eyes are a common feature in monster and ghost traditions worldwide, and the degree to which this motif may influence the perception and reporting of actual eyeshine is difficult to untangle from the biological signal.

Bigfoot's physical outliers are, by comparison, relatively modest, the conical skull shape, the reported sagittal crest, the mid-tarsal break in the foot. These features are unusual in the context of human anatomy but entirely at home in the context of great ape anatomy. Bigfoot's outliers, in other words, are outliers only from a human perspective.

From a primate perspective, they are standard equipment. This is itself a difference worth noting: Bigfoot's unusual features push it toward the known ape lineage, the Mapinguari's push it toward an entirely different mammalian order, and the Yowie's most distinctive feature; the red eye glow, pushes it toward either an unknown primate adaptation or a marsupial physiology that has no close parallel.

These outliers are not evidence against the creatures' existence. They are evidence of the complexity of the phenomenon; a reminder that the accounts we are working with are not clinical field observations produced under controlled conditions, but human experiences filtered through culture, fear, limited visibility, and the fundamental difficulty of describing something that does not fit into any existing category. The outliers are where the data gets messy, and messy data is not bad data. It is simply data that demands more careful interpretation, and more honest acknowledgment of the limits of what the current evidence can tell us.

The Evidence Asymmetry

The three cases are not equally strong, and the differences in their evidence bases reveal as much about the infrastructure of investigation as they do about the creatures themselves.

Bigfoot has the deepest evidence base by a wide margin. Thousands of track casts, the Patterson-Gimlin film, the Sierra Sounds, the Skookum Cast, decades of spectrographic voice analysis, hair and scat samples, and a witness database numbering in the thousands. This depth is not primarily a function of Bigfoot being more real than the other two; it is a function of North America being the wealthiest, most technologically equipped, and most institutionally organized of the three research environments. Bigfoot research has more investigators, more equipment, more funding (however modest), and a larger English-speaking public audience than Mapinguari or Yowie research will likely ever have.

The Mapinguari evidence base is sparse; a handful of track impressions, unconfirmed hair and scat samples, and a body of witness testimony collected primarily by a single dedicated researcher. This sparseness reflects not only the extreme difficulty of conducting fieldwork in the deep Amazon but also the cultural barriers that discourage investigation: indigenous communities that regard the creature as a sacred enforcer are not natural allies to outside researchers setting camera traps in their territory. The physical evidence gap for the Mapinguari is real, but it is at least partially an artifact of the investigation gap; a creature in the most inaccessible habitat on Earth, studied by the smallest and least-funded research community, within a cultural framework that actively resists systematic inquiry.

The Yowie evidence base falls between the other two; more substantial than the Mapinguari's but far thinner than Bigfoot's. Track casts exist but are less rigorously documented. Hair samples have been collected but not subjected to the depth of analysis applied to North American samples. The witness database is smaller, reflecting Australia's lower population density and the smaller community of dedicated investigators. But the Yowie case has something the other two lack: sixty thousand years of continuous oral tradition supporting it, from a culture whose oral histories have been independently verified against the geological and paleontological record.

The evidence asymmetry means that direct comparison of evidence quality across the three cases must be conducted with caution. A creature with more evidence is not necessarily more real than a creature with less; it may simply be more investigated. The comparative method must account for the infrastructure behind the evidence, not just the evidence itself, and must resist the temptation to treat the depth of the Bigfoot evidence base as a standard against which the other two cases are found wanting. Each case must be evaluated against the conditions under which its evidence was collected, and the limitations of those conditions must be factored into the assessment.

Three Habitats, Three Futures

There is one final divergence that operates not in the past but in the present and the future, and it may ultimately determine which of these questions gets answered, if any of them do.

The three habitats in which these creatures are reported face very different futures, and those futures have direct implications for the trajectory of investigation.

Bigfoot's habitat is under moderate pressure. Logging, development, and climate change are reducing the extent and quality of old-growth forest in the Pacific Northwest, but vast wilderness areas remain protected under federal and state management. The infrastructure for investigation; roads, trails, research stations, is the best developed of the three. If Bigfoot exists, the North American wilderness provides both a refuge large enough to sustain a population and an access network that gives researchers a realistic chance of finding evidence. The window of opportunity, while narrowing, remains open.

The Mapinguari's habitat is under severe and accelerating threat. Deforestation in the Brazilian Amazon, driven by agricultural expansion, logging, and infrastructure development, is consuming the deep *terra firme* forests at a pace that has drawn global alarm. The very remoteness that may have protected a relic population for millennia is being eroded by the chainsaw and the bulldozer. If the Mapinguari exists, the forest it depends on is disappearing. The bitter irony, noted in Chapter 2, bears repeating: the creature most likely to be real among the three; the one with the strongest fossil lineage and the most plausible habitat, is also the one whose habitat is most immediately threatened. The window of opportunity is not merely narrowing. It may be closing.

The Yowie's habitat faces a different set of pressures. Deforestation in the Australian eastern ranges has been less dramatic than in the

Amazon, but the continent's escalating fire regime; driven by climate change and exacerbated by decades of fire suppression and land management decisions, poses a different kind of threat. The catastrophic bushfire season of 2019–2020 burned more than forty-six million acres of Australian landscape, much of it in the eastern forests where Yowie reports concentrate. For a population already constrained by habitat fragmentation and low density, a single extreme fire season could be devastating. The window of opportunity is open but fragile. These differing futures mean that the three questions are not equally urgent. The Mapinguari question, if it is ever going to be answered, must be answered soon; before the habitat that makes the answer possible ceases to exist. The Yowie question faces a slower but real erosion of opportunity. The Bigfoot question, by comparison, has more time, but time is not infinite, and the pace of habitat loss accelerates with each decade.

The differences between these three creatures; in body, in behavior, in lineage, in evidence, and in the futures of their habitats are as informative as their similarities. Together, the two chapters paint a picture of a phenomenon that is neither monolithic nor random but patterned; shaped by the same forces that shape every living thing on Earth. Whether the phenomenon is biological, psychological, cultural, or some intersection of all three, it behaves as though it is subject to the rules of the natural world.

That observation does not prove anything. But it is the foundation on which every subsequent chapter builds.

Chapter 6: The Absence That Persists

This is the chapter the book has been building toward, and it would be dishonest to approach it with anything less than full candor.

If a large, unknown animal inhabits the forests of three continents; if the convergent testimony of indigenous cultures, colonial observers, and modern witnesses across North America, South America, and Australia describes something real; then where is the proof? Not the suggestive evidence. Not the intriguing pattern. The proof. The body on the table. The bones in the drawer. The tissue sample under the microscope. The type specimen that transforms a hypothesis into a confirmed species.

It does not exist.

No verified skeleton of any of these creatures has been recovered. No carcass has been submitted to a laboratory and confirmed as belonging to an unknown species. No living specimen has been captured. No DNA sequence from a confirmed sample has been entered into any genetic database. Across three continents, thousands of reported encounters, and more than a century of active investigation, the single piece of evidence that would resolve the question definitively has not materialized.

This absence is not a footnote to the phenomenon. It is the phenomenon's central fact, and it must be confronted at the level of seriousness it deserves. The preceding chapters have established that the testimonial evidence is more specific, more consistent, and more ecologically calibrated than casual dismissal allows. This chapter asks whether that testimonial strength can survive the evidentiary void at its center and, more importantly, whether the void itself can be explained by anything other than the creatures' non-existence.

The strongest version of the skeptical case deserves to be stated plainly before any response is attempted, because intellectual honesty requires engaging with the best arguments against one's position, not the weakest.

The Skeptical Case at Full Strength

The argument against the existence of these creatures is not primarily an argument about any single piece of evidence. It is a cumulative argument about probability, and it runs as follows.

We live in an age of unprecedented technological surveillance of the natural world. North America alone contains an estimated fifty million or more motion-activated trail cameras deployed by hunters, wildlife managers, and conservation researchers. Satellite imagery covers the entirety of the Earth's surface at resolutions sufficient to identify individual trees. Thermal imaging technology can detect the heat signature of a large mammal from the air. Environmental DNA sampling can identify species from water, soil, and air samples without requiring a physical encounter. Acoustic monitoring arrays can record and catalog sounds across entire watersheds. Smartphone cameras are carried by virtually every person who enters the wilderness.

Against this backdrop of surveillance, imperfect and unevenly distributed though it is, the continued absence of definitive evidence for a large-bodied animal on three continents strains credulity. The argument is not that any single technology should have found the creature. The argument is that the cumulative weight of all these technologies, deployed across decades, should have produced at least one unambiguous result. One clear photograph. One confirmed DNA sequence. One set of remains. Something.

The skeptic's position is strengthened by a mathematical reality that the cryptid research community has been reluctant to confront directly. A population of large-bodied animals cannot exist as isolated individuals. It requires a breeding population; a minimum viable population sufficient to maintain genetic diversity and avoid inbreeding depression over multiple generations. For large mammals, population genetics models generally place this minimum in the range of several hundred to several thousand individuals, depending on the species' reproductive rate, generation time, and tolerance for genetic bottlenecking.

If Bigfoot exists in North America, it does not exist as one Bigfoot. It exists as hundreds or thousands of Bigfoots, distributed across a continental range, each one eating, defecating, shedding hair, leaving tracks, breaking branches, and eventually dying. The same is true for the Mapinguari and the Yowie. The question is not whether a single large animal could evade detection. The question is whether an entire population; a species, could do so across decades of increasingly sophisticated surveillance.

That is the argument, and it is a strong one. Any honest treatment of this subject must acknowledge its force before attempting to address it.

The Trail Camera Paradox

The trail camera objection is the most frequently raised and the most intuitively compelling. Millions of cameras. Decades of deployment. Millions of images. No Bigfoot, no Mapinguari, no Yowie. Case closed.

But the intuition is built on an assumption that dissolves under examination: the assumption that trail cameras provide comprehensive surveillance of the wilderness. They do not.

Trail cameras are deployed overwhelmingly along game trails, near clearings, at the edges of food plots, and in areas of known wildlife activity. They are positioned to capture deer, elk, bears, turkeys, and other game species whose movement patterns are well-understood and predictable. The placement logic is simple: put the camera where the animals are known to go, and you will photograph the animals.

This logic works for species that use established trails, that are habitual in their movement patterns, and that are either unaware of or indifferent to the camera's presence. It works poorly; sometimes not at all, for species that are trail-averse, unpredictable in their movements, and capable of detecting and avoiding novel objects in their environment.

The detection rates for even confirmed, common species illustrate the point. Studies of trail camera efficiency for known wildlife show significant gaps. Camera traps deployed in optimal positions for mountain lions in California, a large predator whose population is well-documented, routinely miss the majority of individuals moving through the survey area. A 2018 study in the journal *Ecology and Evolution* found that individual mountain lion detection probability per camera-night averaged below fifteen percent even in high-density areas. If a confirmed, non-evasive large mammal passes undetected through established camera networks the majority of the time, the assumption that a hypothetically more intelligent, more evasive species should be reliably captured requires significant qualification.

The deep wilderness factor compounds the problem. The vast majority of trail cameras are deployed within a few miles of roads, trailheads, and property boundaries because cameras require human access for setup, maintenance, and data retrieval. The most remote wilderness areas: the places where a large, evasive animal would be most likely to spend its time are precisely the areas with the lowest camera density. In the Pacific Northwest, millions of acres of designated wilderness have no trail camera coverage whatsoever. In the Amazon, the concept of trail camera deployment barely applies; the logistics of placing, powering, and retrieving cameras in deep *terra firme* forest are prohibitive for all but the most dedicated and well-funded expeditions. In the Australian bush, camera trap networks exist for wildlife management purposes but are concentrated in areas of known fauna activity, not in the deep gorge systems where Yowie reports concentrate.

The trail camera argument, at its strongest, demonstrates that these creatures do not use the same trails as deer and elk in areas within a few miles of human access points. This is a meaningful observation, but it is considerably less powerful than the claim that trail cameras have surveyed the wilderness comprehensively and found nothing. An additional factor that is rarely discussed: trail cameras produce an enormous volume of false negatives even for their target species; images that are triggered too late, that capture only a blurred edge of a fast-moving animal, or that fail to trigger at all due to sensor limitations, battery failure, or environmental interference. The false-negative rate for trail cameras under field conditions is not trivial. A creature that moves primarily at night, avoids established trails, and is intelligent enough to detect and circumvent unfamiliar objects would compound each of these failure modes multiplicatively.

None of this proves that trail cameras should have failed to capture these creatures. But it demonstrates that the failure to capture them is less statistically informative than the raw camera numbers suggest.

The Smartphone Paradox

A related objection holds that in an age when virtually every person carries a high-resolution camera in their pocket, the continued absence of clear photographic evidence is dispositive. Everyone has a camera. No one has a clear photograph. Therefore the creatures do not exist. This argument has emotional force but limited analytical power, for reasons that become apparent when one considers the actual conditions under which encounters are reported.

The typical encounter, across all three traditions, occurs in dense forest or heavy bush, at dusk or after dark, lasts between five and thirty seconds, and involves a witness whose initial response is not "I should take a photograph" but "I should survive this encounter." The physiological stress response; the adrenaline surge, the narrowing of attention, the fine motor impairment that accompanies sudden fear, is not conducive to the calm, deliberate operation of a camera. Hunters who have spent their careers photographing wildlife describe the difficulty of capturing even expected animals in dense forest at twilight. The notion that a terrified witness encountering something unprecedented should be able to produce a clear, well-lit photograph in under ten seconds is an expectation that fails to account for basic human physiology under stress.

Furthermore, the smartphone camera, despite its impressive resolution, is optimized for well-lit, close-range photography. In low-light forest conditions, at distances beyond twenty or thirty feet, the image quality degrades rapidly. Even the most advanced smartphone cameras produce grainy, indistinct images in the conditions where the majority of encounters occur. The expectation that smartphone technology has solved the photographic problem rests on an idealized model of what that technology can actually do in the field conditions that matter. The photographic evidence that does exist; and it is extensive, comprising thousands of images and videos from North America alone, is overwhelmingly ambiguous. It shows dark shapes in trees, blurred figures crossing clearings, indistinct forms at the edge of visibility. Skeptics correctly note that ambiguous photographs are consistent with misidentification. But they are also consistent with genuine photographs taken under the conditions described: poor light, extreme distance, dense vegetation, and a subject that does not hold still.

The photographic problem is real, and it will only be resolved by deliberate, systematic deployment of professional-grade imaging equipment in areas of sustained activity; not by hoping that a hiker's phone camera produces a National Geographic cover shot during a five-second panic encounter.

The Problem of Bodies

Perhaps the most powerful single argument against the existence of these creatures is the absence of physical remains. Animals die. Bones persist. If a population of large-bodied animals has been living and dying in these forests for centuries or millennia, where are the remains?

The question is fair. The answer is more complex than it initially appears.

The persistence of remains in a forest environment is governed by a cascade of processes; scavenging, decomposition, soil chemistry, water action, insect activity, that operate far more rapidly and thoroughly than most people intuitively appreciate. A large mammal that dies in a temperate forest is typically reduced to scattered bone fragments within weeks by scavengers and insects. In the Pacific Northwest, where acidic soils and heavy rainfall are the norm, bone tissue degrades rapidly; calcium leaches from the matrix, the organic collagen breaks down, and within years rather than decades, all but the densest skeletal elements (teeth, portions of the skull, occasional long bone shafts) have disappeared entirely.

In the Amazon, the process is dramatically faster. Tropical heat, humidity, and the extraordinary density of the decomposer community; bacteria, fungi, insects, and scavengers operating around the clock in an environment optimized for biological recycling, can reduce a large carcass to nothing in a matter of days. The concept of a skeleton persisting on the Amazonian forest floor for any extended period is ecologically naive. The forest consumes its dead with a thoroughness that leaves virtually no trace.

In Australia, the process is intermediate in speed but complicated by fire. The bushfire regime of the eastern forests regularly incinerates surface-level organic material, including any remains that might otherwise persist. Between fire, scavengers, and the acidic soils common to eucalyptus forest, the window during which remains are detectable is narrow.

The key comparison is this: consider how often we find the remains of confirmed, common, large-bodied animals in the wild. How many bear skeletons have you encountered in the woods? How many mountain lion carcasses? How many moose? The answer, for almost everyone, is zero. The remains of large forest mammals are almost never found by casual human observers, and are found only rarely by dedicated researchers, because the decomposition process in forest environments is efficient enough to eliminate remains before they are typically encountered. A study in Yellowstone National Park found that bison carcasses; from an animal weighing up to two thousand pounds, were reduced to scattered, unrecognizable fragments within an average of two to four weeks during summer months.

If the remains of a two-thousand-pound bison can vanish in weeks, the absence of recovered remains from a species that is rarer, more remote, and that may; if it possesses the cognitive capacities attributed to it, engage in some form of conspecific body disposal or avoidance of death sites, is less probative than the raw intuition suggests.

The fossil record presents a related but distinct challenge. Fossilization is not the norm for any animal. It is an extraordinarily rare event that requires specific conditions: rapid burial in fine-grained sediment, mineral-rich groundwater, and geological stability over periods of millions of years. Forest environments are among the worst settings for fossilization on Earth. The floor of a forest is a zone of active biological and chemical decomposition, not sedimentary deposition. The fossil record of forest-dwelling primates generally is sparse compared to that of savanna or aquatic species, and entire lineages of confirmed forest primates are known from only a handful of fragmentary specimens.

The absence of fossil evidence is often cited as though the fossil record were a comprehensive catalog of every species that has ever lived. It is not. It is a deeply biased sample, skewed heavily toward animals that lived in environments conducive to preservation and that existed in sufficient numbers to make fossilization statistically probable. A low-density, forest-dwelling species could easily leave no fossil trace at all, and many confirmed species are known to have done exactly that.

The DNA Question

Environmental DNA represents what many researchers consider the most promising avenue for resolving the cryptid question, and its failure; so far, to produce a confirmed result deserves careful examination.

The principle is straightforward. Every living organism sheds DNA into its environment through skin cells, hair, saliva, urine, feces, and other biological traces. This DNA can be extracted from soil and water samples and amplified through polymerase chain reaction techniques, allowing the identification of species present in a given environment without requiring a physical encounter or a captured specimen. The technology has been successfully used to detect the presence of rare and elusive species in a wide range of habitats, and its sensitivity continues to improve.

If Bigfoot, the Mapinguari, or the Yowie exist as biological organisms, they are shedding DNA into their environments constantly. The question is why that DNA has not been conclusively identified. Several factors complicate the picture. The first is the reference genome problem. Environmental DNA identification works by comparing recovered sequences against a database of known genomes. If the target species is not in the database; if no reference genome exists against which to compare the recovered sequence, then the DNA cannot be identified to species. It can be classified to a higher taxonomic level (order, family, genus), but it cannot be confirmed as belonging to a specific, named species. An eDNA sample from an unknown primate would register as "primate, species unidentified"; a result that, in the absence of a reference specimen, is ambiguous rather than confirmatory.

The second factor is contamination. Human DNA is ubiquitous in the environment, and any sample collected by human researchers in an area visited by humans carries a significant risk of contamination. A result showing "unidentified primate DNA" in a forest environment would face immediate and justified skepticism that the sample was contaminated with human DNA. Distinguishing a genuine unknown primate sequence from human contamination requires a level of analytical rigor; clean collection protocols, multiple independent samples, sequencing of informative genetic regions, that has not always been applied in cryptid eDNA studies.

The third factor is the targeted nature of most eDNA surveys. The majority of environmental DNA studies are designed to detect specific known species; salmon, amphibians, invasive plants, and use primers optimized for those species' DNA. A survey designed to detect salmon will not detect an unknown primate, even if the primate's DNA is present in the sample, because the primers are not designed to amplify that sequence. Broad-spectrum metagenomic surveys, which attempt to characterize all DNA present in a sample, are more promising for cryptid detection but are more expensive, more analytically complex, and less commonly conducted in the relevant habitats.

The fourth factor is degradation. DNA breaks down rapidly in warm, humid environments. In the Amazon, the habitat of the Mapinguari, tropical heat and microbial activity can degrade DNA in soil and water within hours or days of deposition. In the Pacific Northwest, high rainfall and acidic soils accelerate degradation. In the Australian bush, UV exposure and temperature extremes take their toll. The window during which shed DNA remains recoverable is narrow, and a sampling program would need to be both geographically targeted and temporally optimized to capture degradable material before it disappears.

None of these factors make eDNA detection impossible. But they collectively explain why the absence of a confirmed eDNA result to date does not carry the evidentiary weight that it might initially appear to. The technology is powerful, but it has not been systematically deployed in the relevant habitats with protocols optimized for the detection of an unknown large mammal. When it is; if it is, the result, positive or negative, will be far more informative than the absence of results from studies that were never designed to answer the question.

The Modern Surveillance Landscape

Trail cameras and eDNA are not the only technologies relevant to the detection question. The broader landscape of environmental surveillance technology deserves assessment, because the skeptical argument draws much of its force from the general impression that we have made the wilderness transparent; that modern technology has left nowhere for a large animal to hide.

Satellite imagery covers the Earth's surface comprehensively, but its resolution for biological detection is limited. Commercial satellite imagery can resolve objects as small as thirty centimeters, which is sufficient to identify large structures, vehicles, and terrain features, but not individual animals moving under forest canopy. Military-grade imagery offers higher resolution, but it is not available for wildlife surveys and, in any case, cannot penetrate dense canopy. The notion that satellite imagery should have detected these creatures rests on a misunderstanding of what satellite technology can actually see in forested environments.

Thermal imaging: detecting the infrared heat signature of a warm-bodied animal, is more promising and has been deployed in limited Bigfoot research contexts. Forward-looking infrared cameras mounted on aircraft or drones can detect large mammal heat signatures in open or lightly vegetated terrain, but their effectiveness drops sharply in dense forest, where canopy cover absorbs and redistributes thermal radiation. In the Amazon, where the canopy is essentially continuous, aerial thermal imaging is largely useless for detecting ground-level fauna. In the Australian gorge country, steep terrain and dense vegetation create similar limitations.

Drone technology has advanced rapidly and offers potential for systematic survey of remote terrain, but it faces practical limitations that are often overlooked. Battery life restricts flight time. Dense canopy restricts visibility. Noise from rotors may drive evasive animals away from the survey area before detection is possible. And the sheer scale of the habitats in question; millions of acres of forest in each case, means that drone surveys provide coverage of a vanishingly small fraction of the relevant area during any given deployment.

LiDAR: light detection and ranging, can penetrate forest canopy to map terrain and ground-level structures, and has been used to discover previously unknown archaeological sites beneath tropical forest. But LiDAR does not detect living organisms. It maps fixed structures. A moving animal is invisible to LiDAR.

The cumulative picture that emerges from this technology assessment is less reassuring than the popular narrative suggests. We have not made the wilderness transparent. We have developed an impressive suite of technologies, each of which has specific capabilities and specific limitations, and none of which provides comprehensive surveillance of the habitats in question. The areas where these creatures are reported; deep old-growth forest, dense tropical rainforest, rugged gorge country are precisely the environments where every available surveillance technology performs at its worst.

The technological surveillance argument against these creatures is strongest in open, accessible terrain with high human activity; terrain where, not coincidentally, sighting reports are least common. In the terrain where reports concentrate, the argument is substantially weaker than it appears.

The Minimum Viable Population

The population genetics challenge is the most technically demanding aspect of the absence problem, and it cannot be avoided.

A single individual does not constitute a species. A breeding population requires a minimum number of individuals; the minimum viable population, to maintain genetic diversity, avoid inbreeding depression, and sustain reproductive replacement over multiple generations. For large mammals with slow reproductive rates and long generation times, the minimum viable population is typically estimated in the hundreds at minimum, with effective population sizes (the number of individuals actually contributing to reproduction) often being a fraction of the total census population.

For a hypothetical large primate with a generation time of fifteen to twenty years, a reproductive rate comparable to known great apes (one offspring every four to six years per female), and a lifespan of thirty to fifty years, the minimum viable population would likely need to be in the range of five hundred to two thousand individuals to maintain long-term genetic health. This is a significant number. Five hundred to two thousand large-bodied animals is not easy to conceal, even in vast wilderness.

But the number must be weighed against the habitat. The forested wilderness of North America encompasses hundreds of millions of acres. The Amazon basin contains over a billion acres of forest. The eastern Australian ranges, while smaller, still comprise tens of millions of acres of rugged, largely unsurveyed terrain. When a minimum viable population of, say, one thousand individuals is distributed across a habitat of a hundred million acres, the density is one individual per hundred thousand acres; roughly one animal per every 150 square miles. At this density, the probability of an accidental human encounter with any given individual is extraordinarily low, and the probability of finding physical remains in terrain where decomposition is rapid and coverage is sparse is lower still.

The population question does not disappear under this analysis. It remains a real constraint. But the numbers, when examined against the actual scale of the habitats in question, are less devastating to the hypothesis than they initially appear. The question is not whether a thousand large animals could hide in a hundred million acres of forest. The question is whether we have surveyed enough of that forest, at sufficient resolution, to be confident that they are not there. The honest answer is that we have not.

Misidentification: The Strongest Skeptical Weapon

The misidentification hypothesis deserves to be presented at its full strength, because it is, in many respects, the most parsimonious explanation for the sighting data.

For Bigfoot, the primary misidentification candidate is the black bear. Black bears can and do stand upright, sometimes for extended periods. Seen at a distance, in poor light, through dense vegetation, a large black bear standing on its hind legs can present a silhouette that is broadly humanoid; tall, dark, bipedal. The bear misidentification hypothesis accounts for a non-trivial percentage of reported Bigfoot sightings, and any honest assessment of the evidence must acknowledge this.

However, the hypothesis has limits. Bears walking bipedally display a distinctive gait; stiff-legged, short-striding, obviously unstable, that is qualitatively different from the smooth, fluid, long-striding walk described in the majority of close-range Bigfoot encounters. Witnesses who are experienced in bear country; hunters, foresters, wildlife biologists, consistently and specifically distinguish what they observed from a bear. The behavioral repertoire described in many Bigfoot encounters (sustained bipedal locomotion, paralleling, wood knocking, vocalization) has no counterpart in black bear behavior. And in the cases where witnesses were close enough to observe detail, the described facial features, body proportions, and movement patterns do not match ursine anatomy.

For the Mapinguari, the candidate misidentifications are the tapir and the jaguar; the two largest land mammals in the Amazon aside from the creatures in question. Neither species walks bipedally. Neither produces the sustained, low-frequency roar described in Mapinguari accounts. Neither generates the incapacitating stench that is the Mapinguari's most distinctive characteristic. The tapir is a large, stocky animal that could, under conditions of extreme poor visibility, be briefly mistaken for something unfamiliar, but the behavioral and sensory profile described in Mapinguari accounts does not match any known Amazonian species. The indigenous and *seringueiro* witnesses who report the Mapinguari are, in virtually every case, men who know the tapir and the jaguar intimately and who specifically distinguish what they encountered from both.

For the Yowie, the misidentification candidates are even thinner. Australia has no native apes, no native bears, and no native large primates of any kind. The animals available for misidentification: kangaroos, feral pigs, and wombats bear no meaningful resemblance to the creature described. Kangaroos are bipedal but have a body plan, posture, and movement pattern that no competent observer could confuse with a large, stocky, broad-shouldered hominid at close range. The Yowie case is, in this respect, the hardest for the misidentification hypothesis to address, because the candidate pool is essentially empty. Misidentification undoubtedly accounts for some fraction of sighting reports across all three creatures. Bears that look like Bigfoot at a distance. Shadows that coalesce into shapes under the influence of fear and expectation. Unfamiliar animals glimpsed briefly in conditions that prevent clear identification. These cases exist, and their existence does not require extraordinary explanation.

But misidentification as a comprehensive explanation for the entire phenomenon must account for the cases that resist it; the close-range, extended-duration, daylight encounters reported by experienced wilderness professionals who specifically and credibly distinguish what they observed from every known animal in their territory. These cases are a minority of the total sighting pool, but they are not a negligible minority, and they are the cases on which the phenomenon's credibility ultimately rests.

The Hoax Landscape

Hoaxes occur. They have occurred in the history of every cryptid discussed in this book, and their existence is not in dispute.

Ray Wallace likely fabricated some trackways near Bluff Creek. The Patterson-Gimlin film has been claimed, inconclusively, as a hoax by multiple parties. Various photographs and videos have been exposed as deliberate fabrications. In the Yowie field, some track casts are of dubious provenance. The Mapinguari evidence base, while too sparse to have attracted significant hoaxing activity, is not immune to the problem.

The hoax hypothesis, applied selectively to specific pieces of evidence, is both reasonable and, in some cases, almost certainly correct. Applied comprehensively to the entire phenomenon, it requires a more extraordinary claim than is commonly recognized.

A comprehensive hoax explanation must account for thousands of independent reports, from individuals who do not know each other, spread across multiple continents, spanning more than a century, from witness populations that include experienced wilderness professionals with no prior interest in cryptids, no financial incentive to fabricate (and significant social incentive not to), and who report their experiences with a consistent emotional register of reluctance, confusion, and fear.

It must account for the fact that the reported details; the smell gradient, the behavioral gradient, the size gradient, the foot morphology differences are ecologically calibrated in ways that a hoaxer would have no reason or ability to engineer unless the hoaxer possessed a sophisticated understanding of comparative biology, behavioral ecology, and ecogeography.

It must account for the fact that the phenomenon predates the modern era by millennia, embedded in the oral traditions of indigenous cultures across three continents that had no contact with one another and no shared cultural template from which to derive a common form. And it must account for the cost-benefit ratio. Hoaxes require motives like fame, money, entertainment, or malice. The overwhelming majority of witnesses gain nothing and lose credibility by speaking. The cost of long-term, coordinated deception across thousands of independent witnesses, producing ecologically coherent details without apparent coordination, is a model that strains the hoax hypothesis at least as much as the existence hypothesis strains credulity.

Hoaxes explain some of the data. They do not explain all of it. And the residual; the portion of the data that survives the application of the misidentification, hoax, and psychological filters; is where the real question lives.

The Psychological Substrate

One of the most intellectually serious explanations for the hairy humanoid phenomenon lies not in the forest but in the architecture of the human mind, and it deserves to be engaged with the respect it merits.

The human brain evolved under sustained predation pressure. For hundreds of thousands of years, our ancestors lived in environments where large predators were a constant threat, and the cognitive systems that detect, interpret, and respond to that threat are deeply embedded in our neurology. These systems are biased toward false positives; it is better, from a survival standpoint, to see a predator that isn't there than to miss one that is. The result is a perceptual apparatus that is primed to detect agency in ambiguous stimuli, to interpret unclear shapes as threatening figures, and to complete incomplete visual data with threat-relevant imagery.

The upright silhouette: broad shoulders, forward-facing eyes, bipedal posture, is one of the most potent triggers for this threat-detection system. It activates what some researchers have termed "agent detection" circuitry: the neural systems that identify potentially hostile actors in the environment. Under conditions of low visibility, stress, and ambiguity; precisely the conditions that characterize the typical encounter, this circuitry can generate vivid, subjectively convincing perceptions of entities that are not physically present.

This explanation is real, it is grounded in established neuroscience, and it undoubtedly accounts for some portion of the sighting data. The question is whether it accounts for all of it.

The strongest version of the psychological hypothesis predicts that the forms produced by this mechanism should vary widely because the mechanism is filling in ambiguous data with culturally available imagery, and the culturally available imagery differs across cultures. An American might "see" a Bigfoot because Bigfoot is the dominant template for wilderness threat in American culture. An Amazonian indigenous person might see a Mapinguari for the same reason. The mechanism would produce culture-specific forms, not a globally convergent one.

But the data shows convergence. The physical descriptions converge on a specific body plan; not merely "threatening figure" but broad shoulders, long arms, absent neck, flat face, hair-covered body. The sensory details converge, the smell, the sound, the percussive communication. The behavioral patterns converge, graduated deterrence, boundary awareness, nocturnal preference. And the convergences are not random. They are ecologically calibrated, varying with habitat in ways that the psychological hypothesis has no mechanism to produce.

The psychological explanation is powerful for individual encounters. It is less powerful for the phenomenon as a whole, because the phenomenon exhibits the kind of systematic, ecology-tracking variation that a perceptual artifact should not produce. A hallucination does not calibrate its body size to Bergmann's Rule. A false positive does not adjust its territorial behavior to habitat pressure. A pattern-completing brain does not generate foot morphologies suited to local substrate.

The psychological substrate is real. It is part of the picture. But it is not the whole picture, and treating it as such requires ignoring the very patterns that make the phenomenon worth studying.

The Gap That Remains

What remains after all the filters have been applied; after the misidentifications have been subtracted, the hoaxes removed, the psychological artifacts accounted for, and the technological limitations acknowledged, is not proof.

It is a residual.

A body of testimony that is too consistent, too specific, and too ecologically calibrated to be comfortably attributed to error, fabrication, or psychology alone, but that lacks the single piece of physical evidence that would transform it from compelling anomaly to confirmed species.

This residual is the phenomenon's enduring condition. It has persisted for decades. It may persist for decades more. The technology to resolve it exists or is being developed. The habitats that contain the answer, if there is an answer, are still largely intact, though they are shrinking. The question is not whether the residual can be resolved. It is whether anyone with the resources, the institutional support, and the methodological rigor required will commit to resolving it before the window closes.

The absence of evidence is not evidence of absence. This maxim has been repeated so often in cryptid discussions that it has become a cliché, and like most clichés, it is both true and insufficient. It is true that the failure to find something does not prove it does not exist. It is insufficient because, at some point, sustained failure to find something despite genuine effort must lower the probability of its existence. Where that point lies; where absence of evidence begins to shade into evidence of absence, depends on the quality and scope of the search. And the honest assessment of the search conducted to date, across all three habitats, is that it has been neither comprehensive enough nor methodologically rigorous enough to draw definitive conclusions in either direction.

We have not proven these creatures exist. We have not proven they do not. We have established that the question is harder than either side typically acknowledges, and that the tools to answer it are available but have not yet been properly deployed.

The gap persists. And gaps, historically, are where the interesting questions live.

Chapter 7: Methods in the Modern Wild

The demarcation between folklore and formal investigation is methodology. A story transitions into data only when a rigorous structure is applied; when the conditions of observation are documented, the possibility of error is accounted for, and the results are recorded in a form that allows independent evaluation. Without that structure, even the most compelling encounter report remains anecdote. With it, even a null result; a carefully conducted search that finds nothing becomes a data point with measurable value.

Historically, cryptid research has suffered from a lack of standardized protocol. The field has been populated by passionate individuals operating without institutional support, without peer review, and without the methodological training that formal academic programs provide. The result is an evidence base of wildly uneven quality; some material collected with genuine rigor, much of it collected under conditions that would not survive scrutiny in any established scientific discipline. This is not, in most cases, a failure of intent. It is a failure of infrastructure. The tools and methods for conducting this research properly exist. What has been lacking is the institutional framework to deploy them systematically.

This chapter does not propose to solve that institutional problem. It proposes something more modest and more immediately useful: a detailed examination of what proper methodology looks like when applied to this specific problem, what tools are available, how they should be deployed in the three habitats examined in this book, and what evidence standards must be met before any result; positive or negative, can be considered meaningful.

The goal is not to write a field manual. It is to demonstrate that the question "Do these creatures exist?" is, in principle, answerable, and to show what answering it would actually require.

What Success Looks Like: Lessons from Confirmed Discoveries

Before discussing methodology for finding creatures that have not been confirmed, it is worth examining how creatures that *were* eventually confirmed were actually found because the history of species discovery provides a direct template for the work at hand. The saola, a large forest-dwelling bovine in the Annamite Mountains of Vietnam and Laos, was unknown to Western science until 1992. It was not found by a dedicated search expedition. It was found when a survey team from the Vietnamese Ministry of Forestry and the World Wildlife Fund discovered a set of unusual horns in a hunter's house during a biodiversity assessment. The horns did not match any known species. Subsequent investigation, including interviews with local hunters who had known the animal for generations, led to the formal description of *Pseudoryx nghetinhensis*; a two-hundred-pound ungulate that had been living in the mountains within a few hundred miles of Hanoi for its entire evolutionary history.

The kipunji monkey of Tanzania was described to science in 2003, identified initially through field observation by researchers conducting a primate survey in the Southern Highlands. The kipunji had been known to local communities, who had their own name for it, but had never been formally documented. Its confirmation required patient fieldwork in difficult terrain, the integration of local knowledge, and the eventual collection of a specimen from a dead individual found by a local farmer.

The Chacoan peccary, a large pig-like mammal, was known only from Pleistocene fossils and assumed to have been extinct for thousands of years until living specimens were found in the Paraguayan Chaco in 1975 by a researcher who had been told about the animals by local indigenous people and had the scientific training to recognize what they were describing.

The pattern across these discoveries is consistent and instructive. In every case, the animal was already known to indigenous or local populations. In every case, confirmation required the integration of local knowledge with formal scientific expertise. In every case, the discovery occurred not through surveillance technology but through boots-on-the-ground fieldwork in remote terrain, conducted by researchers who knew what to look for and had the methodological training to document what they found. And in every case, the final confirmation came not from a photograph or a footprint but from physical material; horns, a specimen, a carcass, that could be subjected to laboratory analysis.

These precedents define the standard. The investigation of Bigfoot, the Mapinguari, and the Yowie must ultimately produce physical material; tissue, bone, hair with follicular root, or confirmed environmental DNA that can be independently analyzed in a laboratory setting. No amount of photographic evidence, acoustic evidence, or testimonial evidence, however compelling, will cross the threshold of formal taxonomic confirmation. The goal is a type specimen or its genetic equivalent. Everything else is preamble.

The Art of Documentation

The foundational discipline of any field investigation is documentation, and the standards required are more exacting than casual familiarity with the subject might suggest.

Photographic evidence of tracks, structures, or visual encounters must include scale references; a ruler, a known object, or ideally a calibrated scale bar placed adjacent to the subject. The history of cryptid photography is littered with images that are impossible to evaluate because the scale of the subject cannot be determined. The phenomenon known informally as the "blobsquatch"; a dark, indistinct shape in a photograph that could be anything from a large primate to a stump, is almost entirely a product of photographs taken without scale reference, at excessive distance, in poor light, and with no contextual documentation.

A properly documented track find requires a sequence of steps that should be second nature to any investigator but that are, in practice, frequently neglected. The site must be secured before any interaction with the prints; a perimeter established to prevent contamination by human or animal traffic. The prints must be photographed from multiple angles with scale bars before any casting is attempted. The soil composition and moisture content should be recorded, along with ambient temperature, recent weather, and the time elapsed since the prints were likely made. GPS coordinates must be logged with high-precision instruments; not consumer-grade smartphone GPS, which can be accurate only to within ten to thirty feet, but survey-grade equipment capable of sub-meter precision.

Casting itself requires care. Dental stone is preferred over plaster of Paris for its finer grain and greater durability, but the pouring technique matters: too forceful a pour can deform soft soil impressions, obliterating the very details; toe splay, pressure ridges, dermal ridges that give a cast its analytical value. The cast must be allowed to cure fully before removal, labeled immediately with date, time, location, and investigator identity, and stored in a manner that prevents damage during transport.

Chain of custody; the documented record of who has handled a piece of evidence from the moment of collection to the moment of analysis, is a concept borrowed from forensic science, and it is essential in cryptid research for the same reason it is essential in criminal investigation: without it, the provenance of the evidence cannot be verified, and its analytical value collapses. Any hair sample, scat sample, tissue sample, or cast that is submitted for laboratory analysis without a clear chain of custody will be rightly, treated with suspicion by the analysts and dismissed by the broader scientific community, regardless of what the analysis reveals.

These are not exotic requirements. They are standard practice in wildlife biology, forensic science, and archaeology. Their consistent absence from much of the cryptid evidence base is one of the primary reasons that evidence base has failed to gain traction with mainstream science; not because the evidence itself is necessarily fraudulent, but because the documentation standards do not permit independent evaluation of its authenticity.

Acoustic Monitoring: Listening to the Forest

The auditory dimension of these creatures; the vocalizations, the wood knocking, the percussive communication documented across all three traditions, represents one of the more promising and underutilized avenues for systematic evidence collection.

Acoustic monitoring technology has advanced dramatically in the past two decades. Autonomous recording units can be deployed in remote locations and left to operate for weeks or months on battery power, capturing the full acoustic environment across a broad frequency range. The data can be processed using spectrographic analysis software that identifies sounds by their frequency, duration, amplitude, and harmonic structure; allowing the detection and classification of vocalizations that the human ear might miss or misidentify.

But the deployment of acoustic equipment in cryptid research contexts requires a level of methodological discipline that has not always been applied. Environmental baseline recordings must precede any target monitoring sessions. This means running the equipment in the survey area for an extended period before any investigation activity occurs; ideally for days or weeks, to establish a comprehensive catalog of the ambient soundscape: every bird call, every insect chorus, every mammalian vocalization, every mechanical noise from distant roads or aircraft. Without this baseline, any anomalous sound captured during the investigation period is uninterpretable; it may be genuinely unusual, or it may be a perfectly normal component of the local soundscape that the investigator simply failed to recognize.

Directional microphone arrays: configurations of multiple microphones separated by known distances, allow the triangulation of sound sources, determining not only what the sound is but where it is coming from and how far away it is. This capability is critical for evaluating vocalizations, because it allows the estimation of the sound's volume at source; a calculation that can constrain the size of the animal producing it. A vocalization that is loud at a distance of a quarter mile implies a chest cavity and vocal apparatus of considerable size. The same vocalization at fifty feet might be producible by a much smaller animal. Without triangulation, volume at source cannot be estimated, and the analytical value of the recording is significantly diminished.

The habitat-specific challenges for acoustic monitoring are significant. In the Pacific Northwest, the dense conifer canopy absorbs high-frequency sounds, and the ambient noise from wind, rain, and running water can mask low-frequency vocalizations during significant portions of the year. In the Amazon, the acoustic environment is extraordinarily dense; the chorus of insects, frogs, birds, and howler monkeys creates a wall of sound through which any unusual vocalization must be distinguished. In the Australian bush, the acoustic environment is more open but subject to wind interference, and the extreme temperature fluctuations can affect equipment performance. The Sierra Sounds represent the gold standard for what acoustic evidence collection can produce when the conditions are favorable and the equipment is adequate. The recordings made by Berry and Morehead in the Sierra Nevada were captured on reel-to-reel equipment that, while primitive by modern standards, provided sufficient fidelity for meaningful spectrographic analysis. Modern autonomous recording units operating at higher sampling rates, with broader frequency response and lower noise floors, could potentially capture material of far greater analytical value; if deployed in the right locations, at the right times, with proper baseline documentation.

Camera Traps: Strategy Over Saturation

The previous chapter addressed the trail camera paradox at length, demonstrating that the failure of existing camera networks to capture these creatures is less informative than it appears. But the question of how camera traps should be deployed; as opposed to how they typically are deployed, deserves detailed treatment, because the difference between recreational trail camera placement and rigorous research deployment is the difference between hoping for a lucky shot and designing a detection system.

Wildlife studies have established that large, intelligent mammals frequently exhibit neophobia; the avoidance of novel objects introduced into their core territory. Chimpanzees, gorillas, and orangutans all display neophobic responses to camera traps, with documented cases of animals inspecting, avoiding, or destroying research equipment. If the creatures under investigation possess cognitive capacities comparable to the great apes, standard camera trap deployment; mounting a visible device on a tree at eye level along an obvious trail, is precisely the approach least likely to produce results. Research-grade camera trap methodology for elusive species employs several strategies that are largely absent from recreational deployment. Cameras are placed not on established trails but along natural landscape features: ridgelines, stream crossings, saddles between valleys, the edges of clearings, that animals are likely to traverse regardless of trail availability. The cameras are concealed to the greatest extent possible, using natural materials to break up their visual outline. Scent contamination from the installer is minimized through the use of scent-free soaps, gloves, and boot covers, and the approach route is planned to avoid leaving human scent trails leading directly to the camera location. In some research contexts, cameras are left inactive for an extended period after installation, allowing any disturbance caused by the installation to dissipate before active monitoring begins.

The density and duration of deployment matter as much as placement. A single camera on a single tree for a single season is a lottery ticket, not a research design. A grid of cameras deployed across a landscape, maintained over multiple seasons, with overlapping fields of view and coverage of multiple habitat types, constitutes a systematic survey whose null results have genuine statistical meaning. The difference is the difference between anecdote and data.

For cryptid-specific deployment, additional considerations apply. If the target species is primarily nocturnal; as the evidence from all three traditions suggests, cameras must be equipped with infrared flash rather than white flash, which can startle and deter light-sensitive animals. If the target species is intelligent enough to detect and avoid camera traps, some portion of the deployment should use concealed trail-side cameras triggered not by the animal's direct passage but by disturbance sensors (ground vibration, acoustic triggers) that detect the animal's approach from a greater distance. If the target species avoids human scent, cameras should be deployed using methods that minimize human ground contact; ideally installed from elevated positions or using long-handled mounting systems.

None of these techniques are exotic. They are standard practice in the study of rare, elusive wildlife: snow leopards, jaguars, wolverines. Their systematic application to cryptid research habitats has been, to date, minimal. This is not a technological problem. It is a resource and coordination problem.

Environmental DNA: The Molecular Search

Environmental DNA has been discussed in the preceding chapters as both a promising technology and an as-yet-unfulfilled one. This section examines what a properly designed eDNA survey for an unknown large mammal would actually require.

The collection protocol is the first critical variable. Water samples should be collected from streams, pools, and seeps in areas of reported activity, using sterile collection vessels and handled with gloves to prevent human DNA contamination. Soil samples should be collected from track sites, resting areas, feeding locations, and any site where biological traces (hair, scat, mucus) are visually identified. Air sampling: a newer technique that captures DNA shed into the atmosphere on skin cells and respiratory droplets, is a promising addition but remains technically challenging in open forest environments.

Preservation is the second critical variable. DNA degrades rapidly, particularly in warm, humid conditions. Samples must be preserved immediately upon collection; either through chemical fixation (ethanol or commercial DNA preservation buffers) or through cold chain maintenance (keeping samples at or below freezing until laboratory processing). In the Amazon, where temperatures and humidity are extreme, the cold chain requirement presents a significant logistical challenge that must be planned for in advance of any expedition.

The analytical approach is the third critical variable, and it is where the distinction between targeted and broad-spectrum analysis becomes decisive. A targeted eDNA assay; one designed to detect a specific known species, uses primers that bind to DNA sequences unique to that species. This approach is highly sensitive but useless for detecting an unknown species, because no species-specific primers can be designed for an organism whose genome has never been sequenced. Broad-spectrum metagenomic analysis, which sequences all DNA present in a sample and compares it against the full available database of known genomes; is the approach required for cryptid detection. A metagenomic analysis of a water sample from a Pacific Northwest stream would produce a comprehensive inventory of every species whose DNA is present in that water: salmon, deer, bear, human, amphibians, insects, bacteria, fungi. If an unknown primate's DNA were present, it would appear as a sequence that groups phylogenetically with known primates but does not match any species in the reference database. The sequence would be identifiable to order (Primates) or family but not to species; a result that would be extraordinary and that would demand immediate follow-up sampling and independent replication.

The cost of metagenomic analysis is significant; typically, several hundred to several thousand dollars per sample, depending on sequencing depth which limits the number of samples that can be processed and places a premium on strategic collection. Samples should be collected from locations where the probability of the target species' presence is highest: areas of recent reported activity, known track sites, water sources in core habitat areas, and seasonal concentration points (such as the salmon spawning streams hypothesized as Bigfoot attractants in the Pacific Northwest).

A properly designed eDNA survey would collect hundreds of samples across multiple seasons, process them through a metagenomic pipeline optimized for mammalian detection, and apply statistical models to estimate the probability of detection given the sampling density and the assumed population size. The result, whether positive or negative, would carry genuine scientific weight; a standard that no cryptid eDNA study to date has met.

Thermal Imaging and Aerial Survey

Forward-looking infrared cameras and drone-mounted thermal sensors represent the newest additions to the field detection toolkit, and their potential for cryptid research is significant, but their limitations must be understood clearly.

Thermal imaging detects the infrared radiation emitted by warm-bodied objects against a cooler background. A large mammal moving through a forest at night produces a heat signature that is, in principle, detectable at considerable range, particularly against the relatively cool backdrop of the forest floor and vegetation. Handheld FLIR units have been used in limited Bigfoot research contexts, and several investigators have reported capturing thermal signatures of large, bipedal figures moving through forested terrain at distances too great for visual identification.

The limitations are substantial. Dense canopy absorbs and redistributes thermal radiation, reducing the contrast between the target and the background. In warm environments, particularly the Amazon, where ambient temperatures approach the body temperature of a large mammal; thermal contrast drops to near zero. In the Australian bush, the extreme daytime heat radiating from rock surfaces can create thermal clutter that masks biological signatures. Thermal imaging is most effective in cool, open environments precisely the conditions that are least representative of the habitats where these creatures are reported.

Drone-mounted thermal sensors offer the advantage of aerial perspective, potentially looking down through gaps in the canopy rather than through the horizontal clutter of the forest floor. But drone operations in the relevant habitats face practical constraints: limited battery life in cold conditions, restricted flight time in regulated airspace, noise that may drive evasive animals from the survey area before detection, and the fundamental challenge of covering meaningful acreage with a platform whose effective survey range is measured in hundreds of meters per flight.

The most productive application of thermal imaging in this context may not be as a primary detection tool but as a response tool; equipment that can be rapidly deployed to a location where other indicators (acoustic detections, fresh tracks, witness reports) suggest the creature's recent presence. A thermal sweep of the area surrounding a fresh encounter site, conducted within hours of the report, would have a meaningfully higher probability of detection than random aerial survey of the general habitat.

The Indigenous Knowledge Protocol

One of the most underutilized resources in cryptid research, and one of the most sensitive; is the ecological knowledge of indigenous communities who share the landscape with the reported creatures. The precedents from confirmed species discoveries are unambiguous. The saola was known to Vietnamese and Laotian hunters. The kipunji was known to Tanzanian communities. The Chacoan peccary was known to Paraguayan indigenous peoples. In every case, indigenous knowledge was not merely useful but essential to the discovery; it directed researchers to the right habitats, the right seasons, and the right behavioral patterns.

The indigenous communities surrounding all three creatures in this book possess deep ecological knowledge of their respective environments. Aboriginal Australians have sixty thousand years of accumulated observation of the Australian bush. Amazonian indigenous nations have millennia of experience in the most biodiverse forest on Earth. North American indigenous nations have their own deep traditions of ecological knowledge. In every case, these communities report the creature not as a myth but as a component of the local fauna; something that is seen, heard, and avoided according to practical rules of coexistence.

Integrating this knowledge into formal research requires a protocol that respects indigenous sovereignty, acknowledges intellectual property, and avoids the extractive dynamic that has characterized too many interactions between Western researchers and indigenous communities. Informed consent must be obtained before any testimony is recorded or used. Community benefit agreements should ensure that indigenous participants share in any outcomes of the research. Cultural protocols regarding the discussion and depiction of certain beings must be respected; some indigenous communities regard their knowledge of these creatures as sacred and pressuring them to share it for scientific purposes violates both ethical standards and, in many jurisdictions, legal protections.

When this knowledge is ethically obtained and properly integrated, it provides something that no technology can replicate: a multi-generational record of ecological observation conducted by people who have lived in the relevant habitat for centuries or millennia and who possess a granularity of understanding about its fauna, its seasons, and its patterns that no short-term research expedition can match.

Witness Interviews: The Forensic Standard

The witness database is the largest body of evidence available for all three creatures, and its value depends entirely on how the testimony is collected.

Witness interviews in cryptid research must adhere to forensic standards; the same standards applied in criminal investigation, where the accuracy of testimony can determine the outcome of a trial. This is not an aspirational standard. It is a necessary one, because the same cognitive biases that distort testimony in a courtroom operate with equal force in a forest encounter.

Open-ended questioning is the foundational technique. The interviewer asks the witness to describe what happened, in their own words, without prompts or leading questions. "Tell me what you saw" produces more reliable information than "Did you see a large, hairy creature?" because the former allows the witness to retrieve their memory without the influence of external suggestion, while the latter implants details that the witness may unconsciously incorporate into their account.

The timing of the interview matters critically. Memory research has established a well-documented decay curve: the accuracy of recall decreases as the interval between the event and the documentation increases. Interviews conducted within hours of an encounter capture significantly more detail and significantly fewer confabulated elements than interviews conducted weeks or months later. The practical implication is that the cryptid research community needs a rapid-response capability; investigators who can reach a witness location within hours of a report, not weeks.

But the relationship between emotional intensity and memory accuracy is more complex than the simple decay curve suggests. High-stress events are encoded differently than routine experiences. The emotional intensity of the encounter; the fear, the adrenaline, the sense of unreality tends to increase the vividness and confidence of the memory while simultaneously decreasing its precision for peripheral details. A witness may remember the creature's eyes with extraordinary clarity while being uncertain about the time of day or the distance involved. This pattern is well-established in the psychological literature on flashbulb memory, and interviewers must account for it, treating vivid, confident recall of specific features with appropriate caution, and not dismissing uncertain recall of contextual details as evidence of fabrication.

The interviewer must also be trained to recognize and account for post-event contamination, the influence of media exposure, conversations with other witnesses, and exposure to existing cryptid literature on the witness's memory. A witness who has watched Bigfoot documentaries after their encounter may unconsciously incorporate details from those programs into their account, not through dishonesty but through the well-documented process of memory reconstruction. The forensic interview protocol includes specific techniques for identifying and isolating these contamination effects.

Sighting Database Analysis: Mining the Existing Data

One of the most underexploited resources in cryptid research is the existing body of sighting data; thousands of reports, many documented with locations, dates, times, weather conditions, and detailed descriptions that has accumulated over decades.

This data, while of variable quality, is susceptible to statistical analysis that can reveal patterns invisible to case-by-case examination. Geographic clustering analysis can identify hotspot areas with a precision that anecdotal mapping cannot match. Temporal analysis can detect seasonal patterns; correlations between sighting frequency and specific ecological events like salmon spawning, berry ripening, or fire-driven habitat displacement. Weather and lunar phase analysis can test whether encounter rates correlate with conditions that would affect animal activity patterns.

Bayesian occupancy modeling: a statistical framework widely used in wildlife management; can estimate the probability that a species is present in a given area based on detection and non-detection data from surveys. Applied to the sighting database, occupancy modeling could produce probability maps showing which areas are most likely to contain the target species based on the totality of the reporting data. These maps could then direct field resources to the areas with the highest estimated probability of encounter; transforming a scattered, opportunistic search effort into a targeted, data-driven one.

The critical caveat is data quality. Any statistical analysis is only as reliable as the data it operates on, and the cryptid sighting databases contain entries of wildly varying credibility. Applying rigorous filtering criteria excluding reports that lack specific location data, that were made long after the event, that cannot be verified against weather and environmental records, or that show obvious signs of fabrication; would reduce the database size but increase its analytical value. A smaller, cleaner dataset produces more reliable statistical results than a larger, noisier one.

Habitat-Specific Methodology

The three habitats examined in this book present fundamentally different operational challenges, and any serious research program must adapt its methodology accordingly.

In the Pacific Northwest, the primary advantages are accessibility and infrastructure. Roads, trails, and research stations provide access to large areas of wilderness. Equipment can be deployed and maintained with relative ease. The temperate climate is manageable for long-duration fieldwork. The primary challenges are the vast scale of the habitat, the dense canopy that limits aerial and satellite observation, and the high rainfall that degrades both physical evidence and electronic equipment. A research program in the Pacific Northwest would emphasize camera trap grids, acoustic monitoring arrays, systematic eDNA water sampling from streams and rivers, and rapid-response investigation of fresh encounter reports.

In the Amazon, the operational challenges are extreme. Access to the deep *terra firme* forests where the Mapinguari is reported requires multi-day river travel followed by overland penetration through some of the most difficult terrain on Earth. Equipment must be waterproofed, powered by solar panels or high-capacity batteries, and protected from the relentless biological assault of the tropical environment; humidity, insects, fungal growth on electronic components. The heat degrades eDNA samples rapidly, demanding either immediate field preservation or cold chain logistics that are extraordinarily difficult to maintain in a remote forest camp. A research program in the Amazon would emphasize indigenous partnership (the essential foundation without which no deep-forest work is possible), water-based eDNA sampling from the stream networks that drain the *terra firme* blocks, acoustic monitoring during the dawn and dusk periods when vocalization activity is most likely, and systematic collection of trace evidence (hair, scat, tracks) from areas identified by indigenous informants as active zones.

In the Australian bush, the challenges fall between the other two. The eastern ranges are accessible by road in many areas but become extremely rugged in the gorge country where reports concentrate. The fire regime introduces a complication that neither of the other habitats faces: equipment deployed in the bush is at risk of destruction during bushfire events, and the disruption to wildlife patterns caused by fire creates both challenges (displacement of normal fauna that confounds detection) and opportunities (post-fire concentration of survivors at water sources and unburned refugia). A research program in Australia would emphasize camera trap deployment in the deep gorge systems, acoustic monitoring in areas of sustained reporting, thermal imaging during winter months (when thermal contrast is greatest), and close partnership with Aboriginal communities whose knowledge of the bush and its inhabitants is unmatched.

The Expedition That Should Be Mounted

The methodological tools described in this chapter exist. The analytical techniques are proven in other contexts. The habitats, while challenging, are accessible to well-equipped expeditions. The question is not whether the investigation can be done properly. It is whether anyone will do it.

A properly designed detection program for any one of these three creatures would require a multi-disciplinary team: a field biologist to design and manage the survey; a geneticist to oversee eDNA collection and analysis; an acoustics specialist to deploy and interpret audio monitoring; a primatologist or relevant wildlife expert to assess behavioral and ecological evidence; a forensic interviewer to collect witness testimony to evidentiary standards; and, critically, an indigenous liaison or cultural advisor to facilitate ethical partnership with local communities.

The program would need to operate over multiple seasons; a minimum of two to three years of sustained fieldwork, to account for seasonal variation in the target species' behavior and to build a dataset large enough for meaningful statistical analysis. It would need a budget sufficient to cover equipment procurement, laboratory analysis (particularly eDNA metagenomic sequencing), personnel costs, logistics, and data management. A conservative estimate for a serious, multi-year detection program in any one of the three habitats would be in the range of several hundred thousand to several million dollars; a figure that is modest by the standards of wildlife conservation research but entirely beyond the reach of the independent investigators who have historically carried this work.

The institutional barriers to mounting such a program are addressed in a later chapter. For now, it is sufficient to note the irony: the tools to answer the question exist, the methodology to deploy them is well-established, and the cost is within the range of routine scientific research. What is missing is the will; the institutional willingness to invest resources in a question that the scientific establishment has decided, largely without investigation, is not worth asking.

The methods are ready. The question is whether anyone will use them.

Embracing the Null

This chapter closes where it began: with the foundational discipline that separates investigation from advocacy.

The modern investigator must embrace null results. A properly conducted search that finds nothing is not a failure. It is a data point; a quantified statement about what is not present in a given area at a given time, with a measurable level of confidence. Accumulated null results, from well-designed surveys covering substantial habitat, eventually build toward a definitive negative conclusion; the evidence of absence that the previous chapter distinguished from the mere absence of evidence.

Confirmation bias is the true adversary in this field. The desire to find something; the emotional investment in a particular outcome is the force that degrades methodology, inflates ambiguous results, and ultimately undermines the credibility of the entire enterprise. Every investigator who enters the field wanting Bigfoot to be real, wanting the Mapinguari to be a living ground sloth, wanting the Yowie to be confirmed, is an investigator at risk of interpreting shadows as substance and noise as signal.

The antidote is not passion. Passion is necessary; no one endures the physical discomfort, financial sacrifice, and social ridicule of sustained cryptid fieldwork without it. The antidote is discipline. The discipline to record what is observed, not what is hoped for. The discipline to preserve chain of custody even when the finding seems insignificant. The discipline to submit results for independent analysis rather than interpreting them in isolation. And the discipline to accept, if the evidence points that way, that the shadow in the forest is sometimes just a shadow.

The study of the ecological edge requires all of these things. It requires rigor, resources, and patience. But above all, it requires the humility to follow the evidence wherever it leads into the forest, or out of it.

Chapter 8: The Psychology of Encounter

Before we assess what may be lurking in the forest, we must understand the instrument doing the assessing. Every encounter report in this book; every description of a creature's height, build, gait, eye color, and behavioral response was produced by the human nervous system. And the human nervous system is not a neutral recording device. It is a survival machine, shaped by hundreds of thousands of years of predatory pressure, optimized not for accuracy but for speed, and riddled with biases that were useful on the African savanna but that create serious complications for anyone attempting to evaluate the reliability of a witness account in a dark forest in the twenty-first century.

This chapter is not an argument against the existence of the creatures described in this book. It is an argument for understanding the filter through which all evidence for those creatures must pass. The filter is us. And we are complicated.

The Agent in the Shadows

The foundational concept is one that neuroscientists have termed the Hyperactive Agency Detection Device, HADD. This is a cognitive bias, deeply embedded in the human perceptual system, that favors interpreting ambiguous stimuli as intentional agents, predators, people, entities with purpose and awareness rather than as inanimate objects or random environmental events.

The evolutionary logic is straightforward. For a hominid living in an environment populated by large predators, the cost of a false positive; seeing a predator where there is only a shadow, is a moment of unnecessary fear. The cost of a false negative; failing to see a predator that is actually there, is death. Natural selection overwhelmingly favors the system that errs on the side of detection, even at the expense of accuracy. The result is a perceptual apparatus that sees faces in clouds, hears footsteps in settling wood, and interprets the dark shape at the edge of the clearing as something with eyes and intentions.

HADD does not operate in isolation. It is supported by a suite of related mechanisms that, together, create a perceptual environment in which the detection of a large, threatening figure in the forest is not merely possible but, under certain conditions, almost inevitable, whether or not such a figure is actually present.

Pareidolia; the tendency to perceive meaningful patterns, particularly faces, in random or ambiguous visual data is one of these supporting mechanisms. The human visual system is tuned to detect faces with extraordinary sensitivity. Experiments have shown that the face-detection circuitry in the fusiform gyrus of the temporal lobe will fire in response to arrangements of light and shadow that bear only the vaguest resemblance to an actual face: two dots above a line, a pattern of bark on a tree, the configuration of rocks on a hillside. In the dappled light of a forest, where shadows and vegetation create an endless supply of ambiguous visual data, pareidolia provides the raw material from which HADD constructs its agents.

Scotopic vision: the visual mode that dominates in low-light conditions, adds another layer. In darkness, the eye shifts from cone-mediated photopic vision (which provides color and fine detail) to rod-mediated scotopic vision (which provides sensitivity to motion and contrast but sacrifices resolution and color perception). The result is a visual field that is exquisitely sensitive to movement but poor at resolving the details of what is moving. A large, dark shape that shifts position in peripheral vision triggers an immediate orienting response; the head snaps toward the stimulus, the body tenses, the heart rate spikes, but the visual system cannot provide the fine-grained information needed to identify the stimulus before the fear response has already been activated.

This is the perceptual environment in which the majority of close-range encounters across all three traditions occur: low light, dense vegetation, sudden onset, and a nervous system that has already decided the stimulus is a threat before the conscious mind has had time to evaluate it.

The Freeze and What Follows

The physiological response to a perceived threat follows a well-documented cascade that has direct implications for the quality of observation and the reliability of testimony.

The acute stress response: commonly summarized as fight, flight, or freeze is mediated by the sympathetic nervous system and the hypothalamic-pituitary-adrenal axis. Within milliseconds of perceiving a threat, the body releases a surge of adrenaline and cortisol that produces a suite of physiological changes: heart rate increases, blood pressure rises, pupils dilate, non-essential systems (digestion, immune function) are suppressed, and blood flow is redirected to the large muscle groups in preparation for physical action.

These changes have specific and measurable effects on perception and cognition. Attentional narrowing: sometimes called "tunnel vision", focuses the observer's awareness on the perceived source of threat at the expense of peripheral information. A witness in a state of acute stress may have an extraordinarily vivid perception of the creature's face or eyes while being unable to recall the surrounding terrain, the time of day, or whether they were standing or kneeling. This is not a failure of observation. It is the nervous system doing exactly what it evolved to do: prioritizing survival-relevant information and discarding everything else.

Fine motor control degrades. The hands shake. The fingers become clumsy. The act of operating a camera, a phone, or even a flashlight; actions that are trivial under normal conditions becomes disproportionately difficult. This is one of the most frequently overlooked factors in the photographic evidence problem: not that the witness lacked a camera, but that the physiological state produced by the encounter made the camera nearly unusable.

Temporal distortion is another well-documented effect. Under acute stress, the subjective experience of time changes; typically expanding, so that a five-second encounter may be remembered as lasting thirty seconds or more. This distortion is not imaginary. It reflects actual changes in the rate at which the brain encodes perceptual information during high-arousal states. The result is a memory that feels longer and more detailed than the objective duration of the event would seem to allow; a characteristic that can lead investigators to overestimate the quality of the observation and to treat the witness's detailed account as evidence of an extended encounter when the actual visual contact may have been very brief.

The freeze response deserves particular attention in the cryptid context because it is the response most frequently described by witnesses across all three traditions. The witness does not run. The witness does not fight. The witness stands motionless, unable to move, while the creature is observed for what feels like an extended period. This is not cowardice. It is a specific neurological state; tonic immobility, that is triggered by the perception of a threat that is too close and too large to escape through flight. It is the same response that a prey animal exhibits when seized by a predator: a total cessation of voluntary movement, accompanied by heightened sensory awareness and a flood of stress hormones that will later produce an extraordinarily vivid, emotionally intense memory of the event.

The freeze response may, paradoxically, produce the most detailed encounter reports because the witness remains stationary, oriented toward the stimulus, for a longer period than a fleeing witness would. But the detail in those reports is filtered through a perceptual system in crisis mode, and the memory that results is shaped by the emotional intensity of the experience as much as by the sensory data that was actually available.

Memory Under Pressure

The relationship between emotional intensity and memory accuracy is one of the most important and most counterintuitive findings in the psychological literature on testimony, and it has direct relevance to every encounter report in this book.

The common intuition is that vivid memories are accurate memories that the more clearly you remember something, the more likely your memory is to be correct. Research consistently shows that this intuition is wrong. Emotional intensity increases the subjective vividness and confidence of a memory while simultaneously decreasing its accuracy for peripheral details. A witness who remembers the creature's eyes with extraordinary clarity may be genuinely mistaken about its height, its distance, the color of its fur, or the number of seconds the encounter lasted. The vividness is real. The accuracy is not guaranteed.

This phenomenon: known in the literature as the "weapon focus effect" after studies showing that crime witnesses who fixated on a weapon had poor recall of the perpetrator's face has been replicated across dozens of experimental paradigms. Its relevance to cryptid encounters is direct: the witness is fixating on the most threatening and novel element of the experience (the creature) while the surrounding context (distance, terrain, time, ambient conditions) receives diminished processing.

Post-event memory reconstruction adds another layer of complexity. Human memory is not a recording. It is a reconstruction; assembled each time it is accessed from a combination of stored fragments, current emotional state, and available contextual information. Each time a witness tells the story of their encounter, the memory is not merely retrieved but rebuilt, and each rebuilding introduces the possibility of subtle alteration. Details from other sources; conversations with friends, media exposure, subsequent encounters with the research literature can be unconsciously incorporated into the reconstructed memory, not through dishonesty but through the normal operation of the memory system.

This does not mean that witness testimony is worthless. It means that it must be evaluated with an understanding of the mechanisms that shape it. The emotional core of the experience; "I saw something large, bipedal, and covered in hair, and I was terrified", is likely to be more reliable than the specific details; "It was exactly eight feet tall, and its fur was reddish-brown, and it stood there for forty-five seconds." The former is a gross perceptual impression encoded under high arousal. The latter is a set of specific measurements that the visual system, under the conditions described, was almost certainly not equipped to provide with precision.

The Uncanny Valley of the Forest
There is a psychological dimension to these encounters that transcends the mechanics of perception and enters the territory of something deeper; something that may explain not only how witnesses see these creatures but why the experience is so profoundly disturbing.
The uncanny valley: a concept originally proposed in the context of robotics and animation, describes the sharp drop in emotional comfort that humans experience when confronted with an entity that is almost but not quite human. A cartoon character that is broadly humanoid produces no discomfort. A photorealistic digital human that is indistinguishable from a real person produces no discomfort. But an entity that falls in the gap between; one that is close enough to human to trigger recognition but different enough to signal that something is wrong, produces a response of intense unease, revulsion, and fear that is disproportionate to any objective threat.
The creatures described in this book occupy the uncanny valley with extraordinary precision. They are bipedal, like us. They have forward-facing eyes, like us. They have hands, faces, and body proportions that are recognizably primate. But they are too large, too hairy, too broad, and in the accounts of witnesses who have been close enough to see their faces, possessed of an expression that registers as aware, intelligent, and fundamentally *other*. The response this produces in witnesses is consistent across all three traditions: not the fear of a dangerous animal (which is acute but manageable) but a deeper, more visceral dread; a fear that witnesses frequently describe as unlike anything they have experienced before, one that operates at a level

below conscious thought and that persists, in some cases, for years after the encounter.

This uncanny valley response may explain the intensity of the psychological impact reported by witnesses; an intensity that is, in many cases, out of proportion to the actual threat posed by the encounter. The creature did not attack. It did not pursue. In many cases, it simply stood and watched. And yet the witness was left with a psychological imprint comparable to that produced by events of genuine physical danger. The uncanny valley hypothesis suggests that the disproportion is not irrational. It is the nervous system's response to something that triggers the deepest and oldest of human fears: the fear of the almost-human, the not-quite-right, the thing that looks like us but is not us.

The Silence Before the Encounter

Chapter 3 documented a phenomenon reported with striking frequency in Australian Yowie encounters: the sudden, total cessation of ambient sound immediately before or during the sighting. The birds stop calling. The insects go quiet. The forest falls absolutely still. This "silence" phenomenon is not unique to Yowie encounters; it appears in Bigfoot accounts from North America and, less frequently, in Mapinguari reports from the Amazon.

The ecological interpretation: that prey species go silent in the presence of an apex-level disturbance was discussed in Chapter 3 and remains the most parsimonious explanation. But the psychological dimension of the silence is equally important, because it fundamentally alters the perceptual environment in which the encounter occurs.

The ambient soundscape of a forest serves, for the human nervous system, as a continuous signal that the environment is normal. The birds are calling; therefore nothing dangerous is present. This signal is processed below the level of conscious awareness; we do not actively listen for it, but its absence is immediately and powerfully registered. When the forest goes silent, the nervous system interprets the silence as a danger signal; something has changed, something is wrong, and the entire perceptual apparatus shifts into threat-detection mode before any visual stimulus has been detected.

The result is that the witness is already in a state of heightened arousal, with HADD maximally activated and the stress response system primed, before they see anything. The silence pre-loads the encounter. It creates the perceptual conditions under which a large, ambiguous shape in the forest is most likely to be interpreted as a threatening agent; and under which the subsequent memory of that interpretation is most likely to be vivid, emotionally charged, and resistant to re-evaluation.

This does not mean the silence causes the encounter. But it does mean that the silence amplifies it; intensifying both the perceptual experience and the memorial trace in ways that must be accounted for when evaluating the testimony.

The Solo Problem and the Group Dynamic

The majority of close-range encounter reports across all three traditions involve a single witness. This is partly a function of the environments in which encounters occur; deep forest, remote terrain, conditions that favor solitary activity. But the predominance of solo encounters introduces a significant epistemological challenge: there is usually no second observer to corroborate or correct the primary witness's account.

Solo witnesses are more susceptible to the full cascade of perceptual distortion described in this chapter. There is no partner to provide an alternative perspective, no second opinion to check against, no one to say "wait, I think that's a bear." The witness's interpretation of the stimulus is unchallenged in the moment and therefore more likely to crystallize into a firm conviction that is resistant to later re-evaluation. Multi-witness encounters: cases where two or more people independently observe the same event, are less common but more analytically valuable. When they occur, the concordances and discordances between the witnesses' accounts provide a rough measure of perceptual reliability. If two witnesses agree on the gross features of the sighting (large, bipedal, hair-covered) but disagree on specifics (height, color, duration), this suggests that the gross perception is reliable but the specific details are subject to the individual variation predicted by the psychological literature.

The 1977 Blue Mountains confrontation described in Chapter 3 is a useful example. Two witnesses observed the same creature at close range and provided accounts that were broadly consistent in their core features but diverged on specifics. This pattern: agreement on the general, disagreement on the particular, is exactly what the psychology of perception under stress would predict, and its presence in multi-witness encounter reports is, counterintuitively, a mark of credibility rather than a sign of unreliability. Fabricated accounts tend to be suspiciously consistent in their details. Genuine observations under stress tend to converge on the broad picture and diverge on the fine points.

What Psychology Cannot Explain

This chapter has presented, at length and in good faith, the psychological mechanisms that can produce vivid, convincing encounter reports in the absence of an external stimulus. These mechanisms are real. They are well-documented. They operate in every human being who enters a dark forest with an active nervous system. And they unquestionably account for some portion of the sighting data.

But the psychological explanation, powerful as it is, encounters a boundary when it is applied to the phenomenon as a whole and intellectual honesty requires that this boundary be identified as clearly as the mechanisms themselves.

The psychological model predicts perceptual errors that are shaped by cultural expectation. An American in the Pacific Northwest, steeped in Bigfoot media, might be expected to "see" a Bigfoot where a Brazilian rubber tapper, with no such cultural exposure, would see something different or nothing at all. The model predicts culturally specific forms, not a globally convergent one.

The data shows convergence. Not vague, thematic convergence; not merely "people in forests see scary things", but specific, detailed, ecologically calibrated convergence. The same body plan. The same sensory signatures. The same behavioral patterns. Varying in ways that track with habitat rather than culture.

The psychological model predicts that the details of encounters should be most consistent within cultural groups (where the available template is shared) and most variable between them (where the templates differ). The data shows the opposite: the gross features are consistent across cultures while the specific details vary with ecology.

The psychological model predicts that encounter reports should become more similar over time as global media homogenizes the cultural template. The data shows that the core reports; those from indigenous traditions predating modern media are already convergent, and have been for millennia.

The psychological model has no mechanism for generating the smell gradient, the behavioral gradient, the size gradient, or the foot morphology differences documented in the preceding chapters. These are not features that perception under stress would produce. They are features that ecology would produce.

None of this invalidates the psychological model for individual encounters. Some sightings are misperceptions. Some are the product of stress, poor light, and an overactive threat-detection system. The model belongs in the toolkit. But it does not fill the toolkit. And the residual; the portion of the phenomenon that survives the application of the psychological filter, is the portion that requires explanation from a different source.

The mind shapes perception. The environment provides the catalyst. Between those two forces lies the encounter. And the encounter, for all its psychological complexity, continues to produce patterns that psychology alone cannot account for.

Chapter 9: Hidden Populations — Ecological Feasibility

Every large organism leaves an ecological footprint. It eats, it excretes, it sheds hair and skin cells, it disturbs vegetation, it displaces prey, it competes with other species for resources, and it eventually dies, leaving remains that enter the decomposition cycle. The central question of ecological feasibility is not whether a hidden population of large animals *could* exist in a philosophical sense; it is whether the specific habitats in question could sustain such a population at densities low enough to avoid detection while remaining high enough to maintain reproductive viability.

This is a question that can be modeled. Not perfectly, the variables are too numerous, and the target species too poorly characterized for precise calculation, but with enough rigor to establish whether the hypothesis falls within the bounds of ecological possibility or outside them. The preceding chapters have established what these creatures reportedly eat, where they reportedly live, and how they reportedly behave. This chapter takes those parameters and asks what the math says.

The Carrying Capacity Framework

Carrying capacity; the maximum population of a species that a given habitat can sustain indefinitely, is the foundational concept of population ecology. It is determined by the interaction of food availability, water access, shelter, predation pressure, disease, and competition with other species. For any hypothetical population of large-bodied cryptids, the carrying capacity of the reported habitat sets an absolute ceiling on the number of individuals that could exist.

The calculation begins with caloric requirements. A large-bodied mammal's daily energy needs can be estimated from its body mass using well-established metabolic scaling equations. For a mammal in the 400-to-800-pound range; the estimated mass bracket for all three creatures based on witness descriptions and footprint depth analysis, the daily caloric requirement would be approximately 5,000 to 12,000 kilocalories, depending on activity level, ambient temperature, and metabolic efficiency. This is roughly comparable to the caloric needs of a large black bear or a small brown bear.

The next variable is the productivity of the habitat, the amount of usable food energy available per unit area per year. This varies enormously across the three environments, and the variation has direct implications for the population densities each habitat could support.

The Pacific Northwest: The Richest Table

The temperate and boreal forests of the Pacific Northwest are, by the standards of forested ecosystems globally, extraordinarily productive. The combination of high rainfall, moderate temperatures, deep soils, and long growing seasons produces a biomass density that ranks among the highest of any terrestrial ecosystem outside the tropics. The forests generate abundant berry crops (salmonberries, huckleberries, blackberries), extensive root and tuber systems, large populations of ungulates (deer, elk), and critically, the annual salmon spawning runs that flood the river systems with protein of extraordinary caloric density.

The salmon runs deserve particular emphasis because they represent a seasonal resource pulse of a kind that has no equivalent in the other two habitats. During spawning season, millions of individual salmon crowd into shallow waterways throughout the Pacific Northwest, providing a concentrated, predictable, easily accessible food source of enormous caloric value. Black bears in salmon country gain as much as eighty pounds of body mass during the spawning season, building the fat reserves that carry them through winter hibernation. A large, omnivorous primate exploiting the same resource; as the sighting data's seasonal correlation suggests Bigfoot may do, would have access to a caloric windfall capable of sustaining a significantly larger body mass than the forest's baseline productivity alone could support.

Modeling a hypothetical Bigfoot population in the Pacific Northwest using bear analogue parameters produces the following rough picture. Black bears in the Pacific Northwest exist at densities of roughly one individual per five to twenty square miles, depending on habitat quality. A larger, more intelligent, more evasive species; one that actively avoids human contact and camera traps, would be expected to maintain significantly lower densities, both because its larger body size requires a greater home range per individual and because its behavioral strategy of avoidance implies a lower tolerance for conspecific proximity. An estimated density of one individual per fifty to two hundred square miles; roughly a tenth to a fifth of black bear density, would place a hypothetical Bigfoot population across the forested wilderness of the Pacific Northwest, British Columbia, and western Canada (an area of approximately 250,000 to 500,000 square miles of suitable habitat) in the range of 1,250 to 10,000 individuals. The lower end of this range pushes against the minimum viable population threshold discussed in Chapter 6. The upper end is comfortable from a population genetics standpoint but raises questions about detectability; ten thousand large-bodied animals should, in principle, produce more physical evidence than has been documented. The most ecologically plausible estimate is probably somewhere in the middle: a few thousand individuals at very low density across an enormous range, producing encounters at a rate consistent with the sighting database and physical evidence at a rate consistent with the sparse but non-zero record.

The Amazon: The Deepest Refuge

The Amazon basin presents a fundamentally different ecological scenario; one that is, in important respects, more favorable to the concealment of a hidden population than any other habitat on Earth. The raw numbers are staggering. The Amazon contains over two million square miles of forest, of which roughly forty percent; approximately 800,000 square miles, consists of the deep *terra firme* forests where Mapinguari reports concentrate. Large portions of this area have never been surveyed on foot by mammalogists. The biomass productivity of the tropical forest floor is immense, with year-round availability of fruit, foliage, roots, tubers, fungi, and invertebrate protein. For a large-bodied herbivore or omnivore, the food supply is essentially unlimited.

If the Mapinguari is a surviving ground sloth descendant; a large-bodied herbivorous browser with the powerful forelimbs and clawed digits described in witness accounts, its caloric requirements could be met entirely through plant material. A 400-to-600-pound herbivore consuming thirty to fifty pounds of vegetation per day could sustain itself within a home range of five to fifteen square miles of productive *terra firme* forest; a density that, across the available habitat, would support a population numbered in the tens of thousands without approaching the carrying capacity of the ecosystem.

The ecological concealment factors in the Amazon are unmatched. The continuous canopy prevents aerial and satellite detection of ground-level fauna. The rapid decomposition rate eliminates remains within days. The extreme remoteness of the core habitat means that large areas receive zero human survey effort in any given year. The river barriers that segment the basin into isolated blocks create conditions for genetically distinct subpopulations that may never encounter human observers during their lifetimes.

The Amazon's carrying capacity for a hidden megafaunal population is, in short, enormous; large enough that population viability is not the constraint. If the Mapinguari exists, the forest can support it. The constraint is not ecological but evidentiary: the same conditions that make survival possible also make detection extraordinarily difficult.

Australia: The Tightest Margins

The Australian eastern ranges present the most challenging ecological scenario for a hidden population of any of the three habitats, and this must be acknowledged with the same honesty applied to the other cases.

Australia's soils are among the oldest and most nutrient-depleted on Earth. The dominant eucalyptus vegetation is, for most mammals, nutritionally poor and chemically defended. Biomass productivity in the eucalyptus forests of the Great Dividing Range is significantly lower than in the Pacific Northwest or the Amazon; roughly a third to a fifth of the available caloric base per unit area. The implication is direct: a large-bodied omnivore in this habitat would require a much larger home range to meet its caloric needs than its counterparts in richer environments.

The pockets of subtropical and temperate rainforest scattered along the eastern ranges; in the Border Ranges, the Dorrigo Plateau, the Barrington Tops, and the Otway Ranges, represent the highest-productivity zones within the Yowie's reported range, and it is notable that these pockets correspond closely to the areas of densest sighting activity. This correlation between sighting density and habitat quality is precisely the pattern that a real animal would produce and that a culturally driven phenomenon would have no reason to mimic.

Modeling a hypothetical Yowie population requires assumptions about diet that are more speculative than for the other two creatures, given the absence of close ecological analogues in Australia. If the Yowie is a large omnivore exploiting rainforest fruit, creek-system protein (fish, crayfish), small mammals, and marsupial prey, its caloric requirements could be met within home ranges of approximately twenty to fifty square miles in the higher-productivity zones. Across the total available habitat of the eastern ranges; estimated at roughly 40,000 to 60,000 square miles of suitable forest, this density would support a population of roughly 800 to 3,000 individuals.

This is a tight margin. The lower end of the range is below the minimum viable population threshold for long-term genetic health, suggesting that an Australian population would be vulnerable to inbreeding depression, genetic drift, and catastrophic loss from stochastic events; precisely the kinds of pressures that drive small, isolated populations toward extinction.

The catastrophic bushfire season of 2019–2020, which burned over 46 million acres of Australian landscape including significant areas of Yowie habitat, illustrates the vulnerability. For a population already constrained by low density and limited habitat, a single extreme fire season could reduce numbers below the recovery threshold. The Yowie, if it exists, may be the most endangered of the three creatures, not because its habitat is being systematically destroyed, as in the Amazon, but because the margins were always thin and the stochastic risks are high.

Home Range and Dispersal Corridors

Population viability depends not only on total numbers but on connectivity; the ability of individuals to move between subpopulations to maintain gene flow and prevent the genetic isolation that leads to inbreeding depression and eventual population collapse. In the Pacific Northwest, habitat connectivity is relatively strong. The forested ranges of the Cascades, the Coast Ranges, the Rockies, and the vast boreal forests of British Columbia and Alaska form a more or less continuous habitat corridor spanning thousands of miles. A large-bodied, mobile animal could disperse across this range without encountering impassable barriers. This connectivity supports a metapopulation structure; multiple subpopulations linked by occasional dispersal, that is the most robust model for long-term viability.

In the Amazon, connectivity is both aided and constrained by the river systems. The major rivers: the Amazon, the Madeira, the Purus, the Tapajós are formidable barriers to terrestrial dispersal, particularly for an animal that may be unable or unwilling to swim across channels that can be miles wide during the flood season. The *terra firme* forest blocks between these rivers function as ecological islands, each potentially harboring an isolated subpopulation. This island structure would promote genetic divergence between subpopulations; a pattern that, if confirmed through future genetic analysis, could provide evidence of long-term occupancy. But it also means that each subpopulation is more vulnerable to local extinction, because immigration from neighboring populations is limited.

In Australia, the habitat corridor is narrow. The Great Dividing Range provides a north-south axis of connectivity, but the strip of suitable habitat between the settled coastal plain and the arid interior is, in many places, only a few dozen miles wide. Urban development, agriculture, and infrastructure fragment this corridor further, creating bottlenecks that could restrict dispersal and isolate subpopulations. The wildfire regime adds a dynamic element; fire can temporarily sever corridor connections, forcing animals into refugia (typically the deep, moist gorge systems) until vegetation recovers.

The corridor analysis reinforces the picture that emerges from the carrying capacity modeling: the Pacific Northwest offers the most robust conditions for population viability, the Amazon offers the largest total habitat but with significant internal fragmentation, and Australia offers the tightest margins and the most vulnerability to disruption.

Reproductive Constraints

The final part of the ecological feasibility puzzle is reproduction; the rate at which the population replaces itself and the implications of that rate for long-term sustainability.

If these creatures are primates or primate-like animals, their reproductive rate is likely to be slow. The great apes; the closest behavioral and ecological analogues available, reproduce at rates that are, by mammalian standards, extraordinarily low. Female gorillas typically give birth every four to six years. Chimpanzees average one offspring every five to six years. The interval between births is among the longest of any terrestrial mammal, reflecting the high investment that primate mothers make in each offspring; years of nursing, carrying, and social education before the juvenile is independent. A hypothetical large-bodied cryptid primate would face similar reproductive constraints. A female producing one offspring every four to six years, with a sexual maturity age of ten to fifteen years and a reproductive lifespan of perhaps twenty to twenty-five years, would produce four to six offspring over her lifetime. With infant and juvenile mortality rates comparable to those of wild great apes (estimated at twenty to forty percent), the net reproductive rate per female would be approximately two to four surviving offspring. This reproductive rate is sufficient to sustain a stable population under favorable conditions, but it provides almost no buffer against catastrophic loss. A disease outbreak, a severe drought, a catastrophic fire season, or a sustained period of habitat loss could reduce a population faster than its reproductive rate can compensate. The slow reproductive rate of primate-like animals is the primary reason that such populations require large minimum viable numbers: the capacity to absorb losses without declining below the replacement threshold depends on having enough individuals that stochastic events do not extinguish entire age cohorts.

For the Mapinguari, if it is a ground sloth descendant rather than a primate, the reproductive calculus may be somewhat different. Ground sloths' reproductive rates are unknown from the fossil record, but their closest living relatives; the tree sloths, reproduce more slowly even than the great apes, with birth intervals of approximately one to two years but extremely high infant mortality. Adjusting for larger body size and longer development, a ground sloth descendant might have a reproductive profile even more conservative than a primate's, making the population's vulnerability to stochastic loss correspondingly greater.

The Detection Probability Problem

The ecological feasibility question has a mirror image: if a population of the estimated size does exist, what is the probability that it would be detected by the methods currently deployed?

Wildlife management uses a concept called detection probability; the likelihood that a species present in a given area will be detected during a survey of that area. Detection probability is a function of the species' density, its behavior, the survey method's sensitivity, and the amount of survey effort applied. For common, non-evasive species in accessible habitats, detection probability per survey visit can be high, fifty percent or more. For rare, evasive species in difficult terrain, detection probability can be extremely low, single digits per survey effort.

The snow leopard provides an instructive comparison. One of the most elusive confirmed large mammals on Earth, the snow leopard exists at densities of roughly one to ten individuals per four hundred square miles of suitable habitat. Despite decades of dedicated research effort, population estimates remain highly uncertain, individuals are almost never observed directly, and the species was not photographed in the wild until 1971, more than a century after its formal scientific description. Camera trap studies targeting snow leopards in known habitat routinely report detection rates below five percent per camera-station per survey period. If a confirmed, non-mythical species of comparable size and elusiveness is detected at rates this low in habitat where it is known to exist, the failure to detect a hypothetically more evasive species in habitat where its presence is uncertain carries considerably less evidentiary weight than the raw camera numbers suggest.

The wolverine offers another comparison. Wolverines exist at extremely low densities across vast wilderness areas, are primarily nocturnal, actively avoid human contact, and are rarely observed even by experienced wilderness professionals. Despite being a confirmed species with dedicated management programs, wolverines are so difficult to detect that population estimates for entire states are based on the extrapolation of a handful of confirmed sightings and track detections. If wolverines were not already known to science, their detection profile would closely match that of the creatures described in this book.

The detection probability analysis does not prove that these creatures exist. But it demonstrates that the failure to detect them, given the methods currently deployed, the survey effort currently applied, and the behavioral profile consistently described in the testimony, is not the devastating argument against existence that it is commonly assumed to be. The math allows room.

The Outlier Principle

Biology always leaves space for the outlier. The coelacanth was declared extinct for sixty-five million years before a living specimen surfaced in a fisherman's net. The Wollemi Pine, a tree genus known only from fossils dating to the Cretaceous period, was found growing in a remote canyon in the Blue Mountains of Australia in 1994, surviving undetected within two hundred miles of Sydney. The Chacoan peccary was a fossil, then it was alive. The saola was a rumor, then it was real.

The pattern of discovery; from oral tradition to skepticism to confirmation is not a reliable predictor for any individual case. Most rumored species will never be confirmed. Most oral traditions will prove to be purely cultural. The vast majority of cryptid claims will turn out to be misidentification, hoax, or psychology. But the pattern does establish that the ecological argument from improbability is not absolute. Low-density populations in remote habitats have survived undetected for periods that would seem impossible if we did not have the confirmed cases to prove otherwise.

The ecological models presented in this chapter do not confirm the existence of Bigfoot, the Mapinguari, or the Yowie. They confirm something more modest but no less important: that the habitats in question are capable of sustaining populations of the reported size, at densities low enough to be consistent with the current detection record, and with reproductive and dispersal parameters that fall within the bounds of known biological systems.

Existence is possible. Detection is difficult. Confirmation remains elusive. These three statements are not contradictory. They are the ecological condition in which the question persists; and in which the search, if properly conducted, might one day produce the answer.

Chapter 10: The Wider Bloodline

The Global Shadow

The preceding nine chapters have examined three creatures in detail; the Bigfoot of North America, the Mapinguari of the Amazon, and the Yowie of Australia. Their similarities have been mapped. Their differences have been interrogated. The evidence for each has been weighed, and the ecological feasibility of hidden populations in each habitat has been modeled.

But these three do not stand alone.

They are members of a larger family; a global distribution of reported hairy humanoid creatures that spans every major landmass except Antarctica, inhabiting habitats that range from tropical rainforest to alpine snowfield, from temperate deciduous forest to arid scrubland. The creatures vary in size, temperament, and cultural context, but they share the silhouette: bipedal, hair-covered, broadly primate in form, occupying the ecological edge between the human world and the deep wild.

This chapter surveys the wider bloodline; not with the depth that these creatures will receive in future volumes of this series, but with enough detail to establish the scope of the phenomenon and to ask what the global pattern, taken as a whole, suggests about the nature of the signal.

The Yeti: The Roof of the World

The Yeti of the Himalayas is, after Bigfoot, the most widely recognized hairy humanoid in the global imagination and one of the most misrepresented.

The Western popularization of the Yeti as the "Abominable Snowman"; a phrase coined from a mistranslation of a Tibetan term by a British journalist in 1921, has created an image of a creature that inhabits the high, snow-covered peaks of the Himalayas, a white-furred giant stalking the glaciers above the tree line. This image is largely wrong. The indigenous traditions of the Sherpa, Tibetan, and Nepalese peoples describe something quite different: a creature that inhabits the dense rhododendron forests and bamboo thickets of the middle elevations, typically between 8,000 and 14,000 feet, rather than the barren snowfields above. The Yeti is a forest creature, not an alpine one; a distinction that dramatically alters the ecological plausibility of its existence.

The physical description is broadly consistent with the template established in this book, with adjustments for the high-altitude environment. The creature is reported as large; six to eight feet tall, heavily built, covered in dark or reddish-brown hair, and bipedal. The face is described as somewhat flattened, with a pronounced brow ridge. Some traditions describe two distinct types: a larger, more aggressive form and a smaller, more human-proportioned form; a distinction that, if real, might represent sexual dimorphism or, more speculatively, two closely related species occupying different altitudinal niches.

The evidence base includes footprint finds; the most famous being those photographed by Eric Shipton during a 1951 Everest reconnaissance expedition, which show a large, five-toed, humanoid print in snow, hair samples (some of which have been subjected to DNA analysis with inconclusive or contradictory results), and a deep oral tradition extending back centuries in the Himalayan communities. The ecological setting: high-altitude forest with limited human access, rugged terrain, and a biomass base that includes bamboo, berries, and small mammals, is consistent with the requirements of a large-bodied omnivore.

The Yeti will receive full comparative treatment in a future volume of this series, alongside other high-altitude and cold-climate cryptid reports. For the present, it is sufficient to note that its reported characteristics align closely with the global template while its specific adaptations; the high-altitude habitat, the apparent cold tolerance, the physical build, track with local ecology in the same way that the differences between Bigfoot, the Mapinguari, and the Yowie track with theirs.

The Yeren: China's Wild Man

In the remote forests of Hubei Province, in the mountainous center of China, the Yeren; literally "wild man", has been a fixture of local reporting for centuries and a subject of periodic government-sponsored investigation since the 1970s.

The Yeren is described as tall; six to eight feet, with reddish-brown hair covering a muscular, upright body. The face is broad and somewhat human in proportions. The creature inhabits the dense, high-elevation forests of the Shennongjia region, an area of extraordinary biodiversity that serves as a refuge for several other rare species, including the golden snub-nosed monkey and the Chinese giant salamander. The terrain is steep, heavily forested, and sparsely populated, conditions that mirror, in broad terms, the Pacific Northwest habitat of Bigfoot.

What distinguishes the Yeren case is the degree of institutional attention it has received. The Chinese Academy of Sciences organized multiple expeditions into the Shennongjia region during the 1970s and 1980s, collecting hair samples, footprint casts, and witness testimony. The hair samples were analyzed and reported as belonging to an unidentified primate; results that were publicized but never replicated by independent laboratories. Large-scale search expeditions involving hundreds of personnel were mounted, but no specimen was recovered.

The Yeren's geographic position is significant for the fossil lineage question. The Shennongjia region lies within the historical range of *Gigantopithecus blacki*, the enormous fossil ape that is the leading candidate ancestor for Bigfoot. If *Gigantopithecus* or a descendant survived in the forests of central China, the Yeren reports would map precisely onto the expected range. The Yeren case provides what the Bigfoot case lacks: a reported creature in the same geographic region as its proposed fossil ancestor.

The Almasty: The Caucasus Relic

The Caucasus Mountains, stretching between the Black Sea and the Caspian Sea across Georgia, Russia, Azerbaijan, and Armenia, have produced a tradition of reported wild hominids that dates back centuries and that carries a distinct character unlike any of the other cases.

The Almasty; also rendered as Almas, Almasti, or Albasty depending on the language and region, is described not as a giant but as a more modestly proportioned creature, typically five to six feet tall, heavily built but within the range of human variation, and covered in reddish-brown or dark hair. The face is described as more human than apelike, broader and heavier than a modern human's, but recognizably within the hominid range rather than the great ape range. The behavior is typically described as shy and avoidant, though territorial when cornered.

What makes the Almasty case distinctive is the specificity of the descriptions and their potential connection to a different branch of the hominid family tree than the one proposed for Bigfoot. Several researchers, most notably the Russian historian and anthropologist Boris Porshnev, have proposed that the Almasty may represent a surviving population of Neanderthals or another archaic human species; a hypothesis that the physical descriptions, with their emphasis on a robust but fundamentally human-proportioned body, support more naturally than the *Gigantopithecus* hypothesis that dominates the Bigfoot discussion.

The Caucasus is a region of extraordinary linguistic, cultural, and biological diversity; a meeting point of European and Asian fauna, with a history of geographic isolation that has preserved relic species in other taxa. The region's rugged terrain, dense forests, and relatively low population density in the mountain zones provide habitat conditions that are at least superficially consistent with the survival of a small, isolated hominid population.

The Almasty occupies a different position in the comparative framework than the other creatures in this chapter: smaller, more human, potentially closer to our own lineage. Its inclusion in the wider bloodline raises the possibility that the global hairy humanoid phenomenon is not a single species or lineage but a spectrum; from the massive, ape-like Bigfoot at one end to the more modestly proportioned, human-adjacent Almasty at the other, with the Yeti, the Yeren, and others distributed along the continuum.

The Orang Pendek: The Little One

If the Almasty represents the human end of the hairy humanoid spectrum, the Orang Pendek of Sumatra represents something else entirely; a creature whose small size, arboreal behavior, and geographic position suggest a different evolutionary origin altogether. The Orang Pendek; Malay for "short person", is reported from the dense montane forests of the Kerinci Seblat National Park in central Sumatra. It is described as standing three to five feet tall, stocky, covered in short dark or reddish-brown hair, and bipedal on the ground but apparently capable of arboreal locomotion as well. The face is described as broad and somewhat flat. The creature is reportedly shy, avoiding human contact, and is most often encountered by farmers and forest workers at the edges of cultivated areas adjacent to deep forest. The Orang Pendek occupies a unique position in the cryptid landscape because its reported characteristics are consistent with a small-bodied, forest-dwelling ape that is well within the range of known primate diversity. Southeast Asia is the home of the orangutan, the gibbon, and numerous other primate species. The fossil record of the region includes multiple extinct ape species of varying sizes. A small, undiscovered ape in the dense montane forests of Sumatra is not biogeographically implausible in the way that a large primate in Australia is; it falls within the established range of what the region's evolutionary history has produced.

Several serious investigations have been conducted in the Kerinci Seblat area, including expeditions that recovered hair samples and plaster casts of footprints. The hair samples, when analyzed, produced results that were classified as primate but not attributable to any known species, a familiar refrain in cryptid research. The footprints showed a short, broad foot with an apparent divergent big toe, consistent with an ape that combines terrestrial bipedalism with arboreal grasping.

The Orang Pendek is, in many assessments, the most likely of the world's hairy humanoid cryptids to be confirmed as a real species. Its reported characteristics are entirely consistent with known primate biology. Its habitat is a confirmed biodiversity hotspot. Its size places it within the range of animals that could plausibly maintain a viable population in a limited habitat area. If any creature in the wider bloodline is going to be found first, the Orang Pendek is a strong candidate.

The Pattern on the Map

When the wider bloodline is mapped globally, a pattern emerges that is worth examining; not because it proves anything, but because it poses a question that the psychological and cultural explanations must answer.

Hairy humanoid reports cluster along a band of forested habitat that extends, with gaps, around the entire Northern Hemisphere, from the Pacific Northwest across the boreal forests of Canada and Alaska, through the Caucasus, Central Asia, and the Himalayas, into China and Southeast Asia. The Southern Hemisphere entries: the Mapinguari and the Yowie, occupy analogous forested habitats in their respective landmasses. The reports are absent from deserts, open grasslands, tundra, and small islands; environments where a large, forest-dependent animal could not sustain itself.

This distribution pattern is not random. It follows the contours of forested habitat with a fidelity that would be remarkable if the phenomenon were purely cultural or psychological. If hairy humanoid reports were the product of a universal human psychological tendency; the HADD mechanism, the uncanny valley response, the deep-time predator archetype we would expect them to appear in every environment where humans experience wilderness anxiety, including deserts, open savannas, and arctic landscapes. They do not. They appear where forests are, and they disappear where forests end.

The distribution also tracks with known primate biogeography in a suggestive way. The Northern Hemisphere band of hairy humanoid reports overlaps significantly with the historical and current range of the great apes and their fossil relatives. *Gigantopithecus* is known from China and Southeast Asia. Orangutans are native to Borneo and Sumatra. Gorillas and chimpanzees inhabit the forests of equatorial Africa; a continent that, notably, has its own hairy humanoid traditions in the form of the *nkundlunkudlu* of South Africa and the various "pygmy" hominid traditions of Central Africa.

The Southern Hemisphere outliers: the Mapinguari and the Yowie break the primate biogeography pattern, which is exactly why this book chose them for comparative treatment. The Mapinguari's connection to the ground sloth lineage offers a non-primate explanation that fits South American paleontology. The Yowie remains the hardest case; the outlier within the outlier, the creature that should not be where it is.

What the Wider Bloodline Suggests

The existence of a global distribution of hairy humanoid reports does not, by itself, confirm the existence of any individual species. But it does constrain the range of viable explanations.

If the phenomenon is purely psychological; a product of hardwired threat-detection circuitry generating culture-specific monsters, then the global distribution should be random with respect to habitat and should include non-forest environments. It does not.

If the phenomenon is purely cultural; a mythological archetype transmitted between cultures through contact and storytelling, then the distribution should follow trade routes, migration patterns, and cultural exchange networks. It does not. The Aboriginal Australian traditions predate any possible contact with traditions from other continents by tens of thousands of years.

If the phenomenon is biological; if the hairy humanoid reports reflect, even imperfectly, the presence of real animals in real habitats, then the distribution should follow habitat, should vary with local ecology, and should show the pattern of divergent adaptation that characterizes any widely distributed organism. This is exactly what the data shows.

The biological hypothesis does not require that every report represents a real animal. It requires only that the core signal; the persistent, ecologically calibrated, cross-culturally convergent pattern, reflects something that is actually in the forest, however rarely, however imperfectly observed, however heavily overlaid with cultural interpretation and psychological noise.

The wider bloodline does not close the case. But it raises the stakes. A phenomenon that occurs on one continent can be explained locally. A phenomenon that occurs on every major forested landmass on Earth, with the same basic morphology, the same behavioral patterns, and the same ecological calibration, demands either a global explanation or a remarkable series of coincidences.

Future volumes in this series will examine these wider cases in depth; grouping them, as this volume has done, in sets of three for comparative analysis. The Yeti, the Yeren, and the Almasty may form one such grouping. The Orang Pendek and other smaller-bodied reports may form another. Each grouping will apply the same methodology developed in this volume: individual case treatment, followed by systematic comparison, ecological modeling, and honest engagement with both the evidence and its absence.

The bloodline is wider than any single book can encompass. But the method for examining it has been established. And the shadow, wherever the forests reach, continues to watch from the tree line.

Chapter 11: The Noise Problem

Cryptid research does not fail primarily because forests are quiet. It fails because people are loud.

Before any tracks are cast in plaster, before any thermal signature is debated frame by frame, before any sample is sent for environmental DNA testing, an idea has already entered the ecosystem. That ecosystem is not biological. It is social. And its dynamics are governed not by the rules of ecology but by the rules of human communication; rules that favor drama over accuracy, repetition over verification, and narrative satisfaction over empirical restraint.

An alleged creature does not live only in wilderness. It lives in conversation. It lives on screens. It lives in the accumulated weight of every documentary, podcast, television episode, social media post, and campfire story that has ever invoked its name. And once an idea is circulating at that density, it begins to shape its own evidence; not through conspiracy or deliberate fraud, but through the ordinary, well-documented mechanisms by which human cognition interacts with human culture.

The preceding chapters have examined the signal; the patterns in the testimony that resist easy explanation. This chapter examines the noise: the forces that contaminate, amplify, distort, and sometimes manufacture the evidence in which that signal is embedded. Because the signal cannot be properly evaluated until the noise is understood, and the noise, in the case of the great hairy humanoids, is deafening.

The Contamination of Memory

Memory, as Chapter 8 established, is not a static record. It is reconstructive. Each time a memory is recalled, it is rebuilt from fragments; and that rebuilding process is shaped by every piece of information the witness has encountered between the original event and the moment of recall.

In isolated encounters: a lone hiker who sees something unexpected, tells no one for years, and has never watched a Bigfoot documentary; the memory, while subject to the normal processes of decay and reconstruction, is at least free from external contamination. These accounts, when they surface, tend to carry a rawness and a specificity that is qualitatively different from accounts that have been shaped by exposure to the existing literature. The details are sometimes inconsistent with the "standard" description. The creature may be the wrong color, the wrong height, or behaving in ways that do not match the popular template. These inconsistencies, counterintuitively, are markers of credibility; they suggest a memory that has not been smoothed and standardized by contact with the cultural narrative.

In "hotspot" regions: areas where sightings cluster and where the creature has become part of the local identity, the contamination problem becomes acute. Witnesses talk to each other. They compare details. They read local newspaper coverage. They watch documentaries filmed in the very woods where they believe they saw something. They attend community meetings where other witnesses share their accounts. Without any deliberate dishonesty, narratives begin aligning.

A tall, dark shape becomes "seven feet." A fleeting movement becomes "long arms, swinging past the knees." Silence in the forest becomes "intelligence; it knew we were there." Each of these details may have been genuinely observed, or it may have been absorbed from another account and incorporated into the witness's own memory through the normal process of post-event reconstruction. The witness cannot distinguish between the two, because the brain does not flag reconstructed details as different from original perceptions. The memory feels unitary and authentic regardless of its actual composition.

This process operates in all three traditions, but it operates differently in each and the differences are revealing.

In North America, where the Bigfoot cultural template is the most developed and most widely disseminated of the three, contamination risk is highest. A witness in the Pacific Northwest who has an ambiguous encounter in the forest has almost certainly been exposed to Bigfoot media; documentaries, television shows, books, social media content, local folklore. The template is available, and the brain, in the absence of clear perceptual data, will draw on available templates to fill gaps. The result is that the North American sighting database is the largest, the most detailed, and also the most contaminated; a combination that makes statistical analysis both essential and extraordinarily difficult.

In the Amazon, contamination dynamics are different. The *seringueiro* witnesses described in Chapter 2; rubber tappers with no prior exposure to Mapinguari traditions; represent the least contaminated witness class in the entire dataset. Their accounts are valuable precisely because they were produced in a cultural vacuum: men who had never heard of the Mapinguari describing something that independently matched the indigenous accounts. But as Mapinguari stories have circulated more widely through Brazilian media and international cryptid literature, the contamination risk in the Amazon is increasing. Future witnesses will be less culturally isolated than their predecessors, and their accounts will need to be evaluated with correspondingly greater caution.

In Australia, the Yowie occupies an intermediate position. The creature has a lower cultural profile than Bigfoot; fewer documentaries, less merchandising, less media saturation, but it is sufficiently well-known in Australian popular culture that most bushwalkers and rural residents have at least a passing familiarity with the concept. The contamination risk is real but less severe than in North America, and accounts from remote indigenous communities with limited media exposure retain a degree of independence that is becoming increasingly rare in the North American context.

The Television Problem

Television changed cryptid research. Not immediately and not all at once, but irreversibly.

What once existed primarily in newspaper articles, field reports, and privately circulated correspondence now operates in a visual, episodic, drama-driven format. Mystery must be sustained across episodes. Suspense must escalate. Stakes must rise. Dead ends must be reframed as cliffhangers. The rhythm of entertainment requires emotional peaks that the rhythm of investigation does not naturally provide.

Reality programming about cryptids does not require fraud. It requires narrative arc. And narrative arc distorts the practice of investigation in ways that are subtle but cumulative.

Night-vision sequences become performative; the green-tinted visual language of nocturnal investigation carries dramatic weight regardless of what the camera actually captures. Silence becomes dramatic pause rather than data about ambient conditions. Ordinary forest sounds: owl calls, branch cracks, distant coyotes are presented with ominous musical scoring that transforms them into possible evidence. The investigative team's reactions are edited for emotional impact rather than analytical value. And the audience, over hundreds of hours of this formatting, learns to associate cryptid investigation with a specific emotional register; breathless, anxious, perpetually on the verge of discovery, that has nothing to do with the actual experience of careful fieldwork, which is overwhelmingly tedious, uncomfortable, and uneventful.

The feedback loop is the critical mechanism. Witnesses who appear on television, or who watch others appear internalize the performance tropes. Future witnesses unconsciously replicate the language, the pacing, and the emotional cadence they have seen dramatized. An encounter that might have been described in plain, unadorned terms ("I saw something big and dark moving through the trees, and I couldn't identify it") is instead narrated with the rhythms and vocabulary of television ("It was massive; at least eight feet, and it turned and looked right at me, and I knew, I just knew, it was aware of me"). The content may be identical. The packaging shapes how it is received, by the public, by researchers, and by future witnesses who absorb the packaging as part of the template.

A legitimate question must be asked: how many modern sighting reports are unfiltered experience, and how many are experience expressed through a preexisting media lens?

This question does not invalidate reports. It complicates them. And it places a premium on the forensic interview techniques described in Chapter 7; techniques specifically designed to extract the raw perceptual experience from beneath the layers of post-event narrative construction.

The Digital Amplification Engine

The internet compressed the timeline between experience and publication from weeks to seconds, and in doing so, it fundamentally altered the informational ecosystem in which cryptid evidence circulates.

Pre-digital folklore spread locally. A sighting in a small town might reach the regional newspaper, might be picked up by a researcher who happened to be monitoring that paper, and might eventually appear in a book or a newsletter read by a few hundred interested parties. The transmission was slow, the audience was small, and the opportunities for correction and contextualization were numerous.

Digital folklore spreads globally in minutes. An ambiguous photograph can be shared thousands of times before even minimal analysis occurs. Reaction precedes examination. The algorithm rewards engagement, not caution; and engagement is driven by emotional response, which is driven by dramatic framing. A blurry shape captioned "possible misidentification of known wildlife" does not travel as far or as fast as the same shape captioned "undeniable proof; what they don't want you to see."

Over time, repetition produces a phenomenon that might be called manufactured consensus. An image reposted hundreds of times across dozens of platforms feels corroborated, even if its origin remains singular. Each repost is perceived as an independent confirmation, when in reality it is a single data point echoing through a system designed to amplify signal regardless of quality. The result is informational inflation; the subjective sense that the evidence is overwhelming when the actual evidence base may be thin.

The YouTube and podcast ecosystem compounds this effect. Hundreds of channels and programs now produce content about Bigfoot, the Yowie, and related creatures, generating thousands of hours of material annually. The content ranges from serious, investigative work to transparently sensational entertainment, and the audience; particularly the casual audience that forms the bulk of viewership, often cannot distinguish between the two. A carefully researched field report and a staged "encounter" video occupy the same platform, compete for the same attention, and are processed by the same algorithmic ranking system that prioritizes engagement over accuracy.

The serious research community is aware of this problem and has struggled, largely unsuccessfully, to address it. The BFRO's database, which applies filtering criteria to submissions, represents one attempt to impose quality control on the digital flood. But the volume of unfiltered content vastly exceeds the filtered database, and the public perception of the field is shaped far more by the unfiltered content than by the curated material.

The Researcher's Own Noise

The noise problem does not afflict only casual observers and media consumers. It can affect the investigators themselves; and this is perhaps the most insidious form of contamination, because it operates within the very community responsible for distinguishing signal from noise.

Researchers who have dedicated years to fieldwork naturally develop working hypotheses. Those hypotheses are not merely intellectual positions; they are emotional investments. A researcher who has spent a decade investigating Bigfoot has a personal stake in the phenomenon being real that no amount of methodological training can entirely neutralize. The investment is not financial (most cryptid researchers operate at a loss) but psychological: the need to believe that the years of effort, the social cost, the professional marginalization, the physical hardship, have been in pursuit of something that actually exists.

This investment filters perception. If one expects primate behavior, ambiguous movement in the forest may be interpreted as primate-like. If one expects strategic intelligence, silence from the forest may be interpreted as evasive behavior. If one expects wood knocking, a falling branch may be interpreted as a percussive communication. Each interpretation may be correct. But each is also subject to the confirmation bias that the researcher's emotional investment generates.

The strongest investigators recognize this and build controls into their process. Independent observation by team members who do not share findings until documentation is complete. Blind sample collection, where the collector does not know which samples are from "active" areas and which are from control sites. Documentation before discussion; recording what was observed before comparing notes with other team members. These are not exotic techniques. They are standard scientific practice. Their consistent application in cryptid research is the difference between investigation and advocacy.

David Oren, in his Mapinguari fieldwork, applied these controls with unusual discipline; collecting blind samples, documenting witness testimony before sharing it with colleagues, and maintaining a professional skepticism about his own findings that ultimately distinguished his work from that of less rigorous investigators. Jeff Meldrum's track cast analysis follows forensic protocols borrowed from his training in anatomy. These researchers demonstrate that the noise problem is manageable, but only when the investigator acknowledges that they are part of the noise.

The Discipline of Quiet

A mature field of investigation; whether it is called cryptozoology, anomalous primatology, or something else entirely, must embrace a discipline that runs counter to every incentive structure in the modern information environment: the discipline of restraint.

Not every track is authentic. Not every witness is accurate. Not every photograph is useful. Not every sound demands explanation. Not every expedition produces results. And the willingness to say so; publicly, repeatedly, and without apology, is the single most important thing the research community can do to strengthen its own credibility.

The history of cryptid research is littered with evidence that was promoted before it was verified, conclusions that were announced before analysis was complete, and claims that were defended long after they should have been retracted. Each of these episodes; the Wallace foot hoax, the various Patterson-Gimlin costume claimants, the numerous dubious photographs and videos that have been promoted as "proof", damages the credibility of the field as a whole, making it harder for the genuinely anomalous evidence to receive the serious attention it deserves.

The irony is that the discipline of restraint strengthens the residual. A field willing to discard its weakest claims strengthens the credibility of its strongest ones. A researcher willing to say "I don't know what this is, but I cannot confirm it as evidence" commands more respect than one who declares certainty in the face of ambiguity. A community that polices its own standards; that challenges its own members' claims with the same rigor it applies to skeptical objections, builds the kind of credibility that institutions can eventually engage with.

The signal, if it exists, will survive rigorous filtering. If it does not survive filtering, then it was never signal to begin with.

The wilderness is quiet. The internet is not. The future of cryptid research will depend not on louder claims but on quieter discipline, and on the recognition that the noise problem is not something that happens to the field from outside. It is something the field generates from within, and only the field can solve it.

Chapter 12: Translation Errors

Cryptids rarely enter Western literature unchanged. They pass through translation first. And that translation is not only linguistic. It is cultural, philosophical, and sometimes ideological. When stories move from indigenous traditions into anthropological notes, from oral histories into newspaper columns, from spiritual categories into zoological frameworks, something shifts. The shift is not always visible, and it is not always deliberate, but it is always consequential.

A guardian becomes a beast. A boundary marker becomes a monster. A moral tale becomes a biological claim. A being that exists simultaneously in the physical and the spiritual; occupying a category that Western thought does not possess, is forced into one or the other, and the information that does not fit the chosen category is discarded, ignored, or reinterpreted beyond recognition.

If this book is serious about comparative cryptid study; and it is, then it must examine not only whether creatures exist but how the stories about them mutate when they cross cultural borders. Because the evidence base for all three creatures examined in this volume is built, in significant part, on accounts that have been translated, and translation always leaves marks.

The Collision of Categories

In many indigenous traditions, beings described as "wild people," forest guardians, or giant presences are not strictly framed as animals. They occupy a category that has no direct equivalent in the Western intellectual framework; a category that blends physical and spiritual attributes without treating the two as contradictory. The Mapinguari of Amazonian tradition is simultaneously a biological creature that can be seen, heard, and smelled and a transformed shaman whose presence enforces a sacred boundary. The Yowie in certain Aboriginal traditions is simultaneously a physical being that leaves tracks and a Dreamtime entity whose existence is woven into the spiritual fabric of the landscape. The Sasquatch in many North American indigenous traditions is simultaneously a flesh-and-blood neighbor and a being with spiritual properties that place it outside the category of ordinary wildlife.

When outside observers record these accounts; anthropologists, journalists, cryptid researchers, or casual collectors of indigenous lore, they almost invariably filter them through Western categorical thinking. The first question becomes: "What species is this?" The account is evaluated for its zoological content, and the elements that do not fit the zoological framework are either set aside as cultural embellishment or flagged as evidence that the account is "merely" mythological.

But the original narrative may not intend the being to fit into zoological hierarchy at all. The question "What species is this?" may be, from the perspective of the originating culture, not merely unanswerable but meaningless; like asking "What color is Tuesday?" The being exists in a category that the question does not address. This categorical mismatch produces two complementary errors, and both are present in the cryptid literature.

The first error is zoological reduction; stripping the account of its spiritual and cultural dimensions and treating it as a straightforward biological report. This is the error committed by researchers who collect indigenous descriptions of the Mapinguari's physical characteristics (size, fur, smell, tracks) while discarding the transformation narrative, the sacred boundary function, and the second mouth as "superstitious additions." The result is a sanitized zoological profile that is easier to work with scientifically but that may have been shorn of information that is essential to understanding what the tradition actually describes.

The second error is mythological dismissal; concluding that because the account contains spiritual elements, it cannot contain biological information. This is the error committed by skeptics who encounter the shaman transformation narrative in the Mapinguari tradition and conclude that the entire account is obviously mythological, therefore no further investigation is warranted. The spiritual elements are treated as contaminating agents that invalidate the physical descriptions, rather than as a parallel layer of meaning that coexists with the physical content.

The reality, as the indigenous traditions themselves suggest, is that both dimensions may be operating simultaneously, and that the Western insistence on sorting every phenomenon into either the "real" or the "mythological" category may be the actual translation error. The most productive approach, and the one this book has attempted to model, is to maintain both profiles in parallel: the cultural profile (what the being means within its originating tradition) and the zoological profile (what physical patterns appear consistently across accounts). Where the two overlap; where the same physical descriptions appear across cultures whose spiritual frameworks are entirely different, the overlap is where the strongest analytical signal lives.

The Compression of Language

Translation compresses nuance. Words that carry layered meaning in their original language; terms implying "owner of the forest," "wild ancestor," "guardian presence," or "being that walks between worlds" are frequently flattened into singular English approximations such as "monster," "beast," "giant," or "wild man."

That compression alters perception in ways that cascade through the subsequent literature.

Once labeled as a "monster," a being becomes adversarial by default. Its behaviors are reinterpreted as aggression rather than boundary enforcement. Its territorial displays become "attacks." Its vocalizations become "screams" rather than "calls." Its presence in the forest becomes an intrusion to be feared rather than a signal to be respected. Media retellings reinforce this shift with each iteration, and over generations the flattened version becomes the dominant form; the one that new researchers encounter first and that shapes their interpretive framework before they ever access the original source material. The Yowie provides a clear example. The Aboriginal traditions describing this being use terms that carry connotations of power, antiquity, and territorial authority; connotations that are not captured by the English word "Yowie," which carries, through its association with popular culture, connotations of monstrousness and entertainment. A researcher approaching the Aboriginal tradition through the English-language literature encounters the Yowie as a cryptid; a mysterious creature to be investigated. The same researcher approaching the tradition through its original cultural context encounters something considerably more complex: a being whose existence is embedded in a Dreamtime framework that does not separate the physical from the spiritual, the ecological from the sacred. The Mapinguari tradition suffers a more dramatic compression. The word "Mapinguari" itself has been applied, across the literature, to at least two and possibly three distinct beings in Amazonian tradition; a giant ground sloth-like creature, a one-eyed giant, and a transformed shaman. Whether these are three descriptions of the same being, three separate beings conflated under a single name, or a single being with multiple aspects that have been artificially separated by Western categorization is a question that the literature has not adequately addressed. The compression of multiple distinct traditions under a single name creates the illusion of a unified phenomenon that may, in the original cultural context, be considerably more complex.

Colonial Framing and the Hostile Wilderness

Translation errors are not only linguistic. They are also ideological, and nowhere is this more evident than in the colonial literature that forms the earliest Western record of encounters with these creatures. Throughout the period of colonial expansion, in the Americas, in Australia, and across the Pacific, wilderness was frequently portrayed by European writers as hostile, dangerous, and symbolically opposed to civilization. Forests and swamps represented the boundary between the ordered, Christian world and the chaotic, pagan wild. Unknown creatures in these landscapes reinforced that narrative, serving as evidence that the land beyond the settlement line was not merely unmapped but actively threatening.

This ideological framing shaped what was recorded and how. Aggressive encounters were emphasized because they confirmed the narrative of hostile wilderness. Neutral or positive encounters; instances where indigenous communities described coexistence with the creature, or where witnesses reported observation without confrontation were underreported because they did not serve the dominant story. The cumulative effect, visible in the colonial literature of both Australia and the Americas, is that the creatures appear more violent and more monstrous in early European accounts than they do in the indigenous traditions that predate those accounts by millennia. The Yowie's reputation for aggression, which Chapter 3 treated as a genuine behavioral characteristic distinguishing it from Bigfoot, must be evaluated with this colonial filtering in mind. Some of that reputation may reflect real behavioral differences driven by habitat pressure, as the ecological analysis in Chapter 5 proposed. But some of it may be an artifact of colonial reporting bias; a selective emphasis on confrontational encounters that confirmed the European expectation that the Australian bush was a dangerous place full of dangerous things.

Recovering the pre-colonial signal from beneath the colonial overlay is difficult but not impossible. It requires going back to the earliest recorded Aboriginal accounts, working with indigenous communities to access oral traditions that predate European contact, and comparing the content and tone of those traditions with the later colonial records. Where the indigenous traditions describe a creature that is aggressive, and the colonial records agree, the convergence is meaningful. Where the colonial records describe aggression that is absent from the earlier indigenous traditions, the discrepancy should be treated as a possible artifact of the translation process rather than as reliable behavioral data.

Reverse Translation: The Modern Template Problem

Translation errors do not flow only from indigenous culture into Western accounts. They also move in reverse. And this reverse flow may be, in the modern era, the more dangerous of the two directions. Once a global archetype of "hairy upright forest giant" becomes widely recognized; through television, film, books, and the internet, it begins to function as an interpretive template that witnesses and researchers worldwide apply to local phenomena, regardless of whether the template fits.

An unusual primate sighting in Sumatra becomes "Indonesia's Bigfoot." A ground sloth tradition in the Amazon becomes "South America's Sasquatch." An Aboriginal Dreamtime entity becomes "Australia's answer to the Yeti." In each case, the local phenomenon is translated into the language and framework of the global template, and the features that do not fit the template are downplayed or discarded.

This reverse translation flattens genuine diversity. The Mapinguari's possible connection to the ground sloth lineage; a fundamentally different evolutionary hypothesis than the primate hypothesis that dominates the Bigfoot discussion is obscured when the Mapinguari is framed as "a kind of Bigfoot." The Yowie's potential nature as something other than a primate; the convergent marsupial hypothesis, the Pleistocene migration hypothesis is obscured when it is presented as simply the Australian version of a North American phenomenon. The Orang Pendek's small size and arboreal capability; features that distinguish it from every other creature in the wider bloodline are minimized when it is marketed as "the little Bigfoot of Sumatra."

The comparative method that this book employs is designed to resist this flattening. By placing the three creatures side by side and mapping both similarities and differences with equal rigor, the method preserves the distinctiveness of each case while identifying the genuine patterns that connect them. But the method only works if the data it operates on has not already been homogenized by the reverse translation process. The closer we can get to the original, unfiltered accounts; indigenous descriptions recorded in their original languages, early colonial records predating the global Bigfoot template, witness testimony collected before media exposure, the more reliable the comparative analysis becomes.

The Dual Profile Discipline

The practical implication of everything discussed in this chapter is a methodological discipline that must be applied consistently across the entire series: the maintenance of dual profiles for each creature.

The cultural profile documents what the being means within its originating tradition. What role does it play in the cosmology, the oral history, the daily life of the people who have known it longest? What names is it called, and what do those names mean? What behaviors are attributed to it, and what function do those behaviors serve within the cultural framework? What boundaries does it mark, what warnings does it carry, and what relationship does it encode between the human community and the landscape it inhabits?

The zoological profile documents what physical patterns appear consistently across accounts when the cultural framing is set aside. What body plan is described? What size, what proportions, what movement patterns? What sensory details: smell, sound, visual characteristics, recur across independent accounts? What habitat associations are consistently reported? What behavioral patterns repeat?

The overlap between the two profiles is where the most interesting research questions emerge. When morphology, behavior, and habitat converge across cultures with cross-cultural stability; when the zoological profile is consistent even as the cultural profile varies, we move from folklore comparison into pattern analysis. When symbolism and moral function dominate and the physical descriptions are vague or inconsistent, we are likely dealing with narrative continuity rather than species continuity.

The discipline lies in not collapsing one profile into the other prematurely. The zoological profile should not be discarded because the cultural profile contains spiritual elements. The cultural profile should not be stripped away because the zoological profile is the more scientifically tractable of the two. Both must be maintained, compared, and evaluated on their own terms; and the tension between them, rather than being resolved, should be held open as a source of information in its own right.

Translation can distort. But it can also reveal. Where distortion has not erased structural similarity; where the same physical creature is described under different spiritual frameworks, in different languages, by different cultures, something deeper may be present. And recognizing that "something deeper" without forcing it into a premature category is the work that this chapter, and this series, is committed to.

Chapter 13: The Institutional Barrier

If a large, unknown primate were to exist in North America, Australia, or the Amazon, would we expect immediate scientific engagement? The answer, for anyone who understands how scientific institutions actually operate, is no. Not because the question is unworthy of investigation. Not because the evidence is necessarily insufficient to justify preliminary inquiry. But because institutions operate under incentive structures that actively penalize engagement with questions of this kind; and those incentive structures are, in their own way, as much an obstacle to resolution as the forests themselves.

This chapter examines the barrier, not as a conspiracy, which it is not, but as a system of rational self-preservation operating within a professional culture that is structurally incompatible with the investigation of phenomena that have not already been confirmed to exist. Understanding the barrier is essential, because it explains a paradox that has haunted this book from the beginning: the tools to answer the question exist, the methodology is established, the cost is within the range of routine scientific research; and yet the investigation has not been conducted. The reason is not technological. It is institutional.

The Career Calculus

Scientific careers are built upon incremental advancement within established fields. A researcher earns a doctorate by contributing to an existing body of knowledge. They secure postdoctoral positions by demonstrating expertise in a recognized subdiscipline. They obtain tenure by publishing in peer-reviewed journals that serve established research communities. At every stage, the career structure rewards specialization within boundaries that the institution recognizes and values.

A researcher who proposes to investigate the existence of an unknown primate; regardless of how carefully the proposal is framed, how rigorous the methodology, how modest the claims, is proposing to work outside those boundaries. The professional cost of this proposal is immediate, concrete, and well-documented.

Grover Krantz experienced it firsthand. A physical anthropologist at Washington State University with legitimate credentials and a serious publication record, Krantz publicly endorsed the possibility that Bigfoot was a real species in the early 1970s. The consequence was swift: he was denied promotion, marginalized within his department, and treated as a cautionary tale for junior colleagues. His scientific contributions outside the Bigfoot question; contributions that, by any normal standard, would have merited advancement, were evaluated through the lens of his association with a subject that his institution considered disreputable. The message to other researchers was unambiguous: this topic will cost you.

Jeff Meldrum, a professor of anatomy and anthropology at Idaho State University, has experienced a version of the same dynamic. Meldrum's work on Bigfoot foot morphology; rigorous, peer-reviewed, grounded in his expertise in primate locomotion has been met with institutional ambivalence at best and open hostility at worst. His laboratory and his research program exist not because of institutional support but despite institutional discomfort, sustained by his tenure protections and his willingness to absorb professional cost that would deter most researchers.

David Oren, the Harvard-trained ornithologist who pursued the Mapinguari question in the Brazilian Amazon, found that his scientific reputation; built on years of respected work in Amazonian ornithology was retroactively diminished by his association with a cryptozoological subject. The quality of his fieldwork was not questioned. The rigor of his methodology was not challenged. What was challenged was his judgment in choosing to investigate a question that the institution had decided, without investigation, was not legitimate.

The pattern is consistent: the professional cost of engaging with cryptid research falls not on the work itself, which, when conducted by trained scientists, is often indistinguishable in methodology from standard wildlife research, but on the researcher's reputation within a system that evaluates reputation as a proxy for judgment. A scientist who investigates an unknown primate is not seen as someone doing difficult, speculative science. They are seen as someone whose judgment is suspect, and that perception, once established, is nearly impossible to reverse.

The result is a selection effect that removes precisely the people most qualified to conduct the investigation from the pool of available investigators. The researchers with the training, the institutional resources, and the methodological expertise to design and execute a proper detection program are the researchers with the most to lose by attempting it. The researchers who do pursue the question; independent investigators, retired scientists, self-funded enthusiasts are, by definition, those who have either left the institutional system or never entered it, and who therefore lack the resources, the laboratory access, and the professional credibility that the investigation requires.

The Funding Drought

Even if a qualified researcher were willing to accept the career risk, the funding structure of academic science presents a separate and equally formidable barrier.

Scientific research is funded primarily through competitive grants from government agencies, private foundations, and institutional sources. Grant proposals are evaluated by panels of peer reviewers; scientists working in the relevant field, who assess the proposal's scientific merit, methodological rigor, and probability of producing publishable results.

The probability criterion is the killing stroke. A proposal to search for a species whose existence has not been confirmed is, by definition, a proposal with a low probability of producing a positive result. The honest framing: "We are going to spend three years and half a million dollars looking for something that might not be there", is exactly the framing that grant review panels are designed to reject. The funds could be allocated to a project with a higher probability of success, and the panel's fiduciary responsibility to the funding agency demands that they make that allocation.

This creates a perfect catch: without institutional funding, the investigation cannot be conducted at the scale and with the rigor required to produce definitive results. Without definitive results, the investigation cannot attract institutional funding. The cycle stabilizes into a stalemate that has persisted for decades and that shows no sign of breaking through the normal channels of scientific funding.

The few exceptions; Oren's Mapinguari expeditions, funded through his existing institutional position; Meldrum's laboratory work, supported by his university salary; occasional private donations to the BFRO and similar organizations, demonstrate what is possible on a shoestring but do not approach the scale of effort described in Chapter 7's outline of a proper detection program. The multi-disciplinary, multi-year, systematically designed search that the question demands would cost several hundred thousand to several million dollars; a figure that is modest by the standards of wildlife conservation research (a single wolf reintroduction program can cost tens of millions) but entirely out of reach without institutional backing.

The Peer Review Wall

If funding could be secured and research conducted, the results would face another institutional barrier: the peer review system.

Peer review is the mechanism by which scientific claims are evaluated before publication. It is, in principle, a quality control system designed to catch errors, identify weaknesses in methodology, and ensure that published results meet the standards of the field. In practice, it is also a gatekeeping system that reflects the biases, assumptions, and comfort levels of the reviewers.

A paper presenting evidence for an unknown large primate; even a paper with rigorous methodology, properly documented samples, and conservative conclusions, would face an extraordinarily skeptical review process. The reviewers, drawn from established fields (primatology, anthropology, genetics), would bring to the evaluation a prior assumption that the species does not exist. This assumption is not irrational; it is the correct Bayesian prior given the absence of confirmed specimens, but it means that the evidentiary bar for publication would be set far higher than for a paper describing a new subspecies of a known organism or a range extension of an established species.

This elevated bar is not, in itself, unreasonable. Extraordinary claims do warrant extraordinary evidence. But the practical effect is that preliminary or suggestive results; results that, in any other context, would be publishable as contributions to an ongoing investigation are unlikely to survive review in the cryptid context. A paper reporting "unidentified primate DNA in environmental samples from the Pacific Northwest" would be scrutinized for contamination, methodological error, and alternative explanation with an intensity that a paper reporting "novel subspecies of vole identified through eDNA sampling" would not face. The standard is not simply higher; it is categorically different.

The result is that scientific literature contains almost no published research on the question of cryptid existence; not because the research has not been done, but because the results of the research that has been done are not dramatic enough to cross the publication threshold. And the absence of published research is then cited as evidence that the question is not scientifically legitimate; a circular argument that the institutional structure generates and sustains without anyone needing to maintain it consciously.

The Policy Problem

There is a dimension of the institutional barrier that operates not within academia but within government, and it deserves acknowledgment because it introduces incentives that are distinct from the academic career calculus.

Consider the policy implications if a large, unidentified hominid were plausibly confirmed within a managed public land, a national forest, a national park, and a state wilderness area. The confirmation would trigger a cascade of regulatory consequences that no land management agency is eager to initiate.

In the United States, the Endangered Species Act would almost certainly apply. An unknown primate species, by definition rare and potentially endangered, would require a population assessment, a habitat designation, and a management plan. The designation of critical habitat could restrict logging, mining, recreational access, and other activities in areas that may encompass thousands of square miles. Environmental impact assessments for any development project in the region would need to account for the species. Legal challenges from environmental groups, industry stakeholders, and private landowners would follow with certainty.

The economic and political implications are substantial. In the Pacific Northwest, where the spotted owl controversy demonstrated how a single species listing can reshape an entire regional economy, the prospect of a large, charismatic primate requiring habitat protection would be orders of magnitude more disruptive. The timber industry, the recreational industry, and the real estate industry all have interests that would be directly affected.

It is not necessary to posit a conspiracy to recognize that these policy implications create institutional incentives for caution. A land management agency that acknowledges the possibility of an unknown primate in its jurisdiction assumes a burden of investigation, regulation, and public management that it did not seek and may not be equipped to handle. The rational bureaucratic response, and bureaucracies are nothing if not rational in their self-preservation; is to maintain the current position until the evidence is so overwhelming that continued denial is more costly than engagement.

This threshold is very high. And until it is crossed, the institutional silence will persist; not because anyone has been told to be silent, but because silence is the path of least institutional resistance.

The International Dimension

The institutional barrier operates differently across the three research contexts, and these differences have shaped the evidence bases in ways that Chapter 5's analysis of evidence asymmetry only partially captured.

In the United States and Canada, the barrier is primarily reputational. Academic institutions will not fund the research. Peer-reviewed journals will not publish the results. Government agencies will not acknowledge the question. But independent research is not prohibited, and the legal framework permits private citizens to conduct field investigations on public land. The result is a large, active, but informally organized research community operating outside the institutional framework, producing evidence of variable quality that the institutional framework declines to evaluate.

In Brazil, the barrier includes an additional layer: the practical difficulty of conducting any research in the deep Amazon without institutional or governmental support. The remoteness, the logistical complexity, and the cost of deep-forest expeditions effectively require either government permits, institutional affiliation, or partnership with indigenous communities whose cooperation is essential for access. Oren's work was possible because of his position at the Goeldi Museum. Independent researchers without comparable institutional backing face near-insurmountable logistical barriers.

In Australia, the barrier is similar to the North American model; reputational rather than legal, but the smaller size of the research community means that the institutional pressure is more acutely felt. A researcher at a major Australian university who publicly pursued the Yowie question would face the same career consequences as their American counterpart, but in a smaller academic market where alternative positions are fewer and the professional community is more tightly networked.

Breaking the Stalemate

The institutional barrier is not permanent. It is a product of specific incentive structures, and incentive structures can change.

The most likely catalyst for change is a technological breakthrough that produces evidence compelling enough to force institutional engagement; a confirmed eDNA sequence, a clear thermal imaging capture, or a physical specimen. If any of these were produced under conditions of proper documentation and chain of custody, the institutional barrier would not dissolve instantly, but it would begin to crack. The first peer-reviewed paper would face extraordinary scrutiny but would, if it survived that scrutiny, open the door for subsequent work. The first government agency to acknowledge the evidence would face public pressure but would also establish precedent for others. The first funding agency to support a follow-up study would accept risk but would also position itself at the front of what could become a transformative scientific discovery.

The history of science is punctuated by moments when the institutional barrier gave way to the weight of accumulated evidence; sometimes grudgingly, sometimes all at once. Plate tectonics was ridiculed for decades before becoming the foundational framework of modern geology. The bacterial cause of gastric ulcers was dismissed for years before Barry Marshall's self-experimentation forced the medical establishment to reconsider. The discovery of deep-sea hydrothermal vent ecosystems; entire communities of organisms living in conditions that biology had declared impossible was met with astonishment by a scientific establishment that had not predicted or looked for them.

Each of these breakthroughs required evidence strong enough to overcome institutional inertia. The cryptid question has not yet produced evidence of that strength. But the institutional barrier should be understood for what it is; not a verdict on the question's merit, but a structural feature of how science operates when confronted with claims that fall outside its current boundaries. The barrier is real, it is powerful, and it is rational. But it is not impregnable. And understanding its architecture is the first step toward finding the door.

Chapter 14: The Town That Needs a Monster

Not all forces sustaining cryptid belief are biological or psychological. Some are social. Some are economic. And some are so deeply woven into the identity of a place that separating the creature from the community that claims it becomes an act not of scientific clarification but of cultural violence.

This chapter examines a dimension of the cryptid phenomenon that the preceding chapters have touched on but not fully developed: the social and economic structures that form around a reported creature once it becomes part of a community's identity. These structures do not create the creature. They do not, in most cases, involve deliberate fabrication. But they do create conditions under which the creature becomes valuable; symbolically, economically, and psychologically in ways that are independent of its biological status. And that value, once established, generates its own gravitational field, bending the evidence, the investigation, and the public conversation in directions that serve the community's needs regardless of where the truth may lie.

The Anatomy of a Cryptid Town

The pattern is remarkably consistent across communities and continents, and it follows a predictable developmental arc.

It begins with a cluster of sighting reports; a concentration of encounters in a specific geographic area that attracts attention from media, researchers, or both. The attention generates visitors. The visitors generate economic activity. The economic activity generates infrastructure: a festival, a gift shop, a themed hiking trail, a museum, a branded product line. The infrastructure generates identity. And the identity, once established, generates a self-sustaining cycle of attention, visitation, and economic return that persists regardless of whether the sighting reports continue, intensify, or cease entirely.

Willow Creek, California: population roughly 1,700, sits at the gateway to the Bluff Creek drainage where Jerry Crew found the footprints that gave Bigfoot its name and where Patterson and Gimlin shot their famous film. The town has embraced this history with a totality that leaves no corner of the community untouched. A large wooden Bigfoot statue stands at the town's main intersection. The Willow Creek–China Flat Museum maintains a dedicated Bigfoot wing housing track casts, newspaper clippings, and artifacts from decades of local investigation. An annual Bigfoot Days festival draws visitors from across the country. Local businesses sell Bigfoot-themed merchandise: t-shirts, mugs, bumper stickers, carved figurines. The creature's image appears on signage, on storefronts, and in the branding of businesses that have no connection to cryptid research. Fouke, Arkansas: population roughly 800, experienced a similar transformation following the Fouke Monster sightings of the early 1970s, which were dramatized in the 1972 film *The Legend of Boggy Creek*. The film, shot on a minimal budget using local residents as actors, became an unexpected commercial success and established Fouke as a Bigfoot destination. The town's identity shifted accordingly, and decades later the Fouke Monster remains the community's most recognizable cultural export.

In Australia, the Blue Mountains towns west of Sydney: Katoomba, Springwood, Blackheath, have a more complex relationship with the Yowie, one that reflects the creature's lower cultural profile compared to Bigfoot. The Yowie is present in the region's identity but has not achieved the economic dominance it holds in places like Willow Creek. It appears in local art, in hiking trail lore, and in the occasional themed business, but it coexists with the region's other identity markers; the Three Sisters rock formation, the scenic railway, the broader Blue Mountains tourism brand. The Yowie is a thread in the tapestry rather than the whole cloth.

In the Amazon, the economic dynamics operate differently because the communities where the Mapinguari is reported are, in most cases, too remote and too economically marginal to support a tourism infrastructure. The creature has not been commercialized in the way that Bigfoot has. But it serves an analogous social function: it is a marker of the community's relationship to the deep forest, a shared reference point that distinguishes the people who live at the edge of the wild from those who do not. The Mapinguari's value to these communities is not economic. It is existential; a confirmation that the forest they depend on for their livelihood is still deep enough and wild enough to contain something beyond human knowledge.

Economic Incentive Without Malice

The commercialization of a cryptid does not require fraud. It requires only popularity. And popularity, once established, creates economic structures that are self-reinforcing.

A gift shop owner in Willow Creek does not need to believe that Bigfoot is real in order to sell Bigfoot merchandise. They need only to recognize that visitors come to Willow Creek because of Bigfoot, and that visitors who come to Willow Creek will buy Bigfoot-related products. The economic incentive operates independently of the truth value of the underlying claim. The creature is valuable as a brand, as an attraction, as a reason for people to stop in a small town that they would otherwise drive through without slowing down.

This creates a subtle but significant pressure on the community's relationship to the evidence. Disproving the creature; or even expressing skepticism about it, threatens income. Reinforcing the creature; or at least maintaining an atmosphere of mystery and possibility, sustains the economic activity that the community has come to depend on. The pressure is not typically conscious or deliberate. No one in Willow Creek is sitting in a back room plotting to suppress skeptical evidence. But the social environment is one in which enthusiastic engagement with the mystery is rewarded and skepticism is, at minimum, unwelcome.

The effect on evidence quality is predictable. In communities where the creature has become economically important, the threshold for accepting a sighting report as credible drops. Ambiguous evidence is more likely to be promoted than scrutinized. Witnesses who report encounters receive positive social reinforcement; attention, community status, a sense of participating in something meaningful while witnesses who express doubt or retract their accounts face social cost. The incentive structure does not manufacture encounters, but it does create an environment in which encounters are more readily reported, less critically evaluated, and more quickly absorbed into the community's narrative.

Identity at the Edge

The economic dimension, significant as it is, does not capture the full picture. There is a deeper layer; one that operates in communities where the creature has no significant economic value, where no festivals are held and no merchandise is sold, and where the creature's importance is entirely symbolic.

Urban populations interact with wilderness through recreation. Rural populations live beside it. And for communities that exist at the boundary between the settled world and the wild; the logging towns of the Pacific Northwest, the farming communities at the forest edge in the Amazon, the small bush towns of the Australian ranges; the wilderness is not a place they visit. It is a presence they coexist with, a force that shapes their daily lives, and a source of both sustenance and danger.

A cryptid in such a landscape symbolizes the edge of control. It becomes shorthand for a truth that the community knows from daily experience: *there are still things here that are not mapped, not managed, and not understood.* The creature is a living expression of the community's relationship to the land; a relationship that is more intimate, more complicated, and more honest than the relationship that urban populations have with the same landscape.

In this context, the creature serves as a cultural boundary marker. It expresses, in a single vivid image, the community's awareness that the land they live on is not fully known, and their pride in living at the edge of the unknown rather than at the safe center of the known. The creature is theirs in a way that it is not the city's, not the university's, and not the government's. It belongs to the people who live close enough to the forest to have heard it, seen it, or at least to know someone who has.

This identity function is powerful, and it operates independently of the creature's biological status. A community may not need its monster to be real. It may need its monster to *matter*; to serve as a symbol of the community's distinctiveness, its relationship to the land, and its resistance to the homogenizing forces of modernization that threaten to make every place the same as every other place.

Monsters as Meaning Systems

Throughout history, monsters have absorbed anxieties. They have given form to fears that were too diffuse, too abstract, or too socially uncomfortable to be expressed directly. The dragon that guards the hoard. The sea serpent that marks the edge of the navigable world. The werewolf that embodies the fear of the animal within the human. Each monster serves a function within the culture that produced it, and that function persists regardless of whether the monster is biologically real. The cryptids in modern settings sometimes operate in the same way. They absorb anxieties about environmental degradation; the creature that may go extinct before it is confirmed, a loss that would represent the ultimate failure of stewardship. They absorb anxieties about economic decline, the mystery that brings visitors and revenue to a community that has lost its other industries. They absorb anxieties about cultural displacement; the indigenous tradition that is validated by the creature's continued presence and invalidated by its absence. They absorb anxieties about the loss of wildness itself; the fear that there is nothing left in the world that is genuinely unknown, genuinely beyond human control, genuinely other.

These sociological functions must be distinguished from zoological possibility, but they cannot be ignored. They are part of the phenomenon. They shape the evidence, the reporting, the investigation, and the public conversation. A researcher who enters a cryptid community without understanding the social and economic forces at play is a researcher who will misread the data, interpreting social reinforcement as independent corroboration, interpreting economic incentive as investigative enthusiasm, and interpreting community identity as scientific commitment.

The town that needs a monster is not lying. It is doing something more subtle and more human: it is holding onto a story that gives it meaning, and the meaning is real even if the monster is not. Distinguishing the meaning from the evidence; honoring both without confusing the two, is one of the most delicate tasks the serious cryptid investigator must perform.

The Investigator's Obligation

There is an ethical dimension to this chapter that should not be left implicit.

A researcher who enters a community that has built its identity around a cryptid carries an obligation that goes beyond data collection. The community has shared something; its stories, its experiences, its sense of itself, and the researcher must handle that sharing with respect, regardless of what the data ultimately reveals.

This does not mean suppressing skeptical conclusions. It means delivering them honestly, directly, and with acknowledgment of what the community stands to lose; not just economically but socially and psychologically. A researcher who debunks a community's creature without understanding what the creature meant to the community has done only half the work. The other half is recognizing that the loss of a mystery is itself a kind of loss, and that the people who bear that loss deserve to be treated not as dupes who were fooled but as participants in a phenomenon that is more complex than any single explanation can capture.

The town that needs a monster deserves the truth. It also deserves the compassion to receive that truth in a context that acknowledges the full scope of what the monster meant, not just as a biological hypothesis, but as a story, a symbol, a source of pride, and a marker of a community's relationship to the wild.

Chapter 15: Toward a Cryptid Taxonomy

If this series is to develop intellectual consistency across multiple volumes; examining dozens of reported creatures from every major habitat on Earth, it requires structure. "Unknown creature" is not a useful analytical category. It is a waiting room, and waiting rooms do not organize themselves.

The cryptid literature has historically treated all unconfirmed creatures as members of a single, undifferentiated class. Bigfoot is discussed alongside the Loch Ness Monster. The Orang Pendek shares shelf space with Mothman. The Mapinguari is filed next to the Chupacabra. The implicit assumption is that these phenomena are related by their shared status as "things that haven't been proven to exist"; a categorization that is about as analytically useful as grouping a dolphin, a submarine, and a hallucination under the heading "things seen in the ocean."

The result is confusion. Arguments that apply to one type of claim are misapplied to another. Evidence standards appropriate for a zoological hypothesis are demanded of a phenomenon that may be better understood as cultural. Analytical frameworks designed for megafaunal survival are applied to reports that may describe something psychological. The conversation generates more heat than light because the participants are, in many cases, arguing about fundamentally different kinds of things while using the same vocabulary.

This chapter proposes a taxonomy; not of species, since none have been confirmed, but of claims. The taxonomy organizes reported cryptids into functional families based on the nature of the claim being made, the type of evidence that would be relevant to evaluating it, and the analytical framework best suited to the investigation. It is not definitive. It will need revision as the series develops. But it provides a starting point for disciplined comparative analysis, and it prevents the most common analytical error in the field: treating all cryptids as if they were the same kind of question.

Type I — Relict Hominoids and Primate Analogues

The first and most extensively studied category encompasses creatures whose reported characteristics are consistent with an unknown primate; a large-bodied, bipedal or semi-bipedal, hair-covered hominoid inhabiting forested wilderness.

Bigfoot, the Yowie, the Yeti, the Yeren, the Almasty, and the Orang Pendek are the primary entries in this category, and the three creatures examined in this volume; with the Mapinguari as a partial exception, have served as the foundation for its analytical framework. The category is defined not by the assertion that these creatures are primates but by the observation that their reported characteristics align most closely with primate biology and that the investigative methods most likely to resolve their status are those drawn from primatology, physical anthropology, and primate ecology.

The evaluation criteria for Type I claims are the most developed in the field, because this is the category that has received the most sustained investigative attention. Locomotion biomechanics: the analysis of gait, stride length, and foot morphology, provides a framework for assessing track evidence and film footage. Caloric feasibility modeling estimates whether the reported habitat could sustain a population of the reported size. Breeding population modeling determines the minimum number of individuals required for long-term viability. Acoustic analysis evaluates vocalization recordings against the known vocal ranges of primate species. Environmental DNA protocols target primate genetic markers in soil and water samples.

The key analytical challenge for Type I claims is distinguishing between three competing hypotheses: that the reports describe a real, undiscovered primate species; that they describe a real but misidentified known species (typically a bear); or that they describe a perceptual phenomenon with no biological basis. The comparative method developed in this volume; placing multiple Type I creatures side by side and examining their similarities and differences against ecological predictions, is designed to discriminate among these hypotheses more effectively than single-case analysis can.

Type II — Megafaunal Survivors

The second category encompasses creatures whose reported characteristics are most consistent with a species believed to be extinct; a surviving remnant of a lineage that the fossil record documents but that conventional paleontology considers to have vanished.

The Mapinguari is the primary entry in this category from the current volume, with its proposed connection to the giant ground sloths of the Pleistocene. But the category extends well beyond South America. Mokele-mbembe, the alleged surviving sauropod dinosaur of the Congo basin, is the most widely known Type II claim. The thylacine, or Tasmanian tiger, occupies a more modest position; a recently extinct species (last confirmed specimen died in 1936) for which ongoing sighting reports from Tasmania and mainland Australia suggest the possibility of survival. Various lake and river cryptids around the world have been interpreted as surviving plesiosaurs, giant fish, or other aquatic megafauna.

The evaluation criteria for Type II claims differ from Type I in important ways. The fossil record provides a defined physical template against which witness descriptions can be compared; a luxury not available for Type I claims, where the proposed ancestor (*Gigantopithecus*, for example) is known from fragmentary remains that do not permit detailed physical reconstruction. Extinction timelines provide a temporal framework: a species that was last documented eleven thousand years ago (like the ground sloths) is a more plausible survivor candidate than one that was last documented sixty-five million years ago (like the non-avian dinosaurs). Habitat refuge analysis assesses whether the reported habitat could have provided the isolation and ecological continuity necessary for long-term survival.

The key analytical challenge for Type II claims is assessing the probability that a specific lineage survived a documented extinction event. This requires integrating paleontological evidence (what the extinct animal looked like and how it lived), ecological modeling (whether the current habitat could sustain a descendant population), and biogeographic analysis (whether the reported location falls within the extinct species' historical range). The Mapinguari case, as this volume has demonstrated, performs well on all three criteria; the descriptions match the fossil record, the Amazon provides plausible refuge habitat, and the geographic overlap is precise. Other Type II claims fare less well, and the taxonomy allows each to be evaluated against the appropriate standards rather than being lumped with claims that face entirely different evidentiary challenges.

Type III — Aquatic Unknowns

The third category encompasses creatures reported from lakes, rivers, and coastal waters; the vast domain of aquatic cryptids that has generated some of the most famous and most frustrating cases in the field.

The Loch Ness Monster is the archetype, but the category includes lake monsters from around the world: Ogopogo of Lake Okanagan, Champ of Lake Champlain, Nahuelito of Nahuel Huapi Lake in Argentina, and dozens of others. Oceanic cryptids: sea serpents, giant octopuses, and various unidentified marine animals, occupy the same category, though the investigative challenges differ significantly between enclosed lake environments and the open ocean.

The evaluation criteria for Type III claims center on the physics and ecology of aquatic systems. Water depth and volume determine whether the body of water could physically contain an animal of the reported size. Prey biomass modeling estimates whether the food web could sustain a population of large predators. Sonar mapping provides a direct detection method that has no equivalent in terrestrial cryptid research. Water temperature, oxygen levels, and seasonal dynamics constrain the range of organisms that could survive in a given body of water.

The key analytical challenge for Type III claims is that the aquatic environment makes both detection and misidentification fundamentally different from their terrestrial counterparts. Water distorts perception; waves, currents, light refraction, and surface conditions can transform ordinary objects and animals into extraordinary-seeming forms. Logs, otters, swimming deer, and boat wakes have all been documented as sources of lake monster reports. At the same time, the depth and opacity of many lake environments mean that a large animal could, in principle, avoid surface detection for extended periods.

This volume has not examined aquatic cryptids, and future volumes that do will need to develop analytical frameworks specific to the aquatic context. The taxonomy flags this as a distinct category to prevent the error of evaluating lake monsters against the same criteria used for forest-dwelling hominoids; an error that the undifferentiated "cryptid" category encourages.

Type IV — Aerial Unknowns

The fourth category encompasses reports of large flying creatures that fall outside the known range of living avian or chiropteran species. The most widely reported entries in this category include the Thunderbird of North American indigenous and modern tradition; a bird of enormous wingspan reported across the continent, and various pterosaur-like creatures reported from Papua New Guinea, Africa, and the Americas. The Kongamato of Zambia and the Ropen of Papua New Guinea are among the most discussed cases.

The evaluation criteria for Type IV claims draw on aerodynamics, ornithology, and paleontology. Aerodynamic feasibility analysis determines whether an animal of the reported wingspan and body mass could achieve and sustain flight in the atmospheric conditions of the reported location. Roosting habitat assessment evaluates whether the terrain provides nesting and resting sites suitable for a large aerial species. Migratory plausibility examines whether the creature's reported movement patterns are consistent with the seasonal resource availability and atmospheric conditions that govern the migration of known large birds.

The key analytical challenge for Type IV claims is that the aerodynamic constraints on large flying animals are severe and well-understood. The largest confirmed flying bird: the wandering albatross, with a wingspan of up to eleven and a half feet, achieves its size through adaptations specific to oceanic soaring that are not available to terrestrial flyers. Terrestrial birds face more stringent constraints, and the upper limit for powered terrestrial flight in the current atmosphere is generally estimated at wingspans of ten to twelve feet. Reports of aerial creatures significantly larger than this face a physics problem that biological adaptation alone may not overcome.

Type V — Liminal Entities

The fifth and most controversial category encompasses reports whose characteristics include overtly supernatural, paranormal, or reality-defying attributes; creatures that do not behave in ways consistent with any known biological framework and that may be more productively analyzed through cultural, psychological, or phenomenological lenses than through zoological ones.

Mothman, the Skinwalker, the various "black-eyed children" reports, and certain categories of shadow figures fall into this group. These phenomena share a common feature: they are reported by witnesses who describe them in terms that blend physical presence with properties that violate physical law; teleportation, luminescence without a visible source, physical transformation, or association with other anomalous phenomena such as UFO sightings or poltergeist activity.

The evaluation criteria for Type V claims are fundamentally different from those applied to the other four categories. The zoological framework that governs Types I through IV is largely inapplicable, because the reported phenomena do not behave in ways that zoology can model. Cultural analysis: examining the being's function within its originating tradition, its symbolic significance, and its relationship to other cultural narratives becomes the primary analytical tool. Psychological analysis: examining the witness's perceptual and cognitive state, the conditions under which the encounter occurred, and the neurological mechanisms that might produce the reported experience provides a complementary framework.

The inclusion of Type V in the taxonomy is not an endorsement of the paranormal. It is a recognition that some reported phenomena are better served by cultural and psychological analysis than by zoological investigation, and that forcing them into a zoological framework distorts both the phenomena and the framework. A Mothman sighting evaluated against primate ecology standards is an analytical absurdity. A Bigfoot sighting evaluated against paranormal phenomenology standards is equally absurd. The taxonomy prevents both errors by routing each claim to the analytical framework best equipped to address it.

The Boundaries Between Types

The boundaries between these categories are not always sharp, and some creatures straddle them in ways that are analytically productive. The Mapinguari, as this volume has demonstrated, occupies the boundary between Type I (primate analogue) and Type II (megafaunal survivor). Its reported behavior and body plan are broadly hominoid, but its proposed evolutionary lineage connects it to an entirely different mammalian order. This boundary position is not a weakness of the taxonomy; it is one of its most useful features, because it forces the investigator to evaluate the creature against two sets of criteria simultaneously and to assess which framework provides a better fit for the available evidence.

The Yowie straddles the boundary between Type I and something that resists easy categorization. If it is a primate that crossed from Southeast Asia during the Pleistocene, it is a straightforward Type I case. If it is a convergent marsupial that independently evolved a primate-like body plan, it is something that the taxonomy does not yet have a clean category for; a possibility that suggests the taxonomy itself will need refinement as the series examines more cases.

Some creatures may shift categories as evidence accumulates. The thylacine, currently a Type II claim (megafaunal survivor), would shift to "confirmed extant species" if a living specimen were found, removing it from the cryptid taxonomy entirely. A creature currently classified as Type V might, if compelling physical evidence emerged, be reclassified as Type I or Type II. The taxonomy is designed to be dynamic, reflecting the current state of the evidence rather than imposing a permanent classification.

Why This Matters

Classification disciplines enthusiasm. It prevents the most common and most damaging analytical error in cryptid research: the conflation of fundamentally different kinds of claims.

If a claim fits Type I, it must be evaluated under primate ecology; caloric modeling, population genetics, locomotion biomechanics not under folklore narrative alone. If it fits Type II, it must be evaluated against the fossil record and extinction timeline, not against the primate framework that governs Type I. If it fits Type V, forcing it into a zoological framework may be not merely unproductive but actively misleading.

The taxonomy does not prove the existence of anything. It clarifies arguments. It ensures that evidence is evaluated against appropriate standards. It prevents the skeptic from dismissing a Type I claim by pointing to the absurdity of a Type V claim, and it prevents the enthusiast from defending a Type V claim by citing the evidence for a Type I case. It keeps the categories separate so that the patterns within each category, if they exist, can emerge clearly.

Future volumes in this series will classify their subjects within this framework before beginning comparative analysis, ensuring that each grouping contains creatures that face the same analytical questions and that can be meaningfully compared. The first volume has examined two Type I cases and one Type I/II hybrid. Future volumes will explore other combinations; three Type II cases, perhaps, or a Type I alongside a Type III and a Type V, testing whether the analytical frameworks hold up when the categories are mixed.

The taxonomy is a tool. Like all tools, it will need sharpening as it is used. But it provides something that the field has lacked: a structure for thinking clearly about a subject that has, for too long, been discussed as though clarity were the enemy of mystery.

It is not. Clarity is what allows mystery to be taken seriously.

Chapter 16: One Root, Many Branches

This book began with a fish.

The coelacanth: hauled from the depths off South Africa in 1938, sixty-five million years after the textbooks declared it extinct, served as a reminder that the distance between what we know and what exists has never been as small as we assume. The Introduction promised that this book would sit in that distance, examining three creatures that occupy the space between confirmed species and comfortable dismissal. Fifteen chapters later, the question is whether that space has been clarified, narrowed, or merely illuminated.

The honest answer is: all three.

The space has been clarified. The three creatures examined in this volume: Bigfoot, the Mapinguari, and the Yowie, are not interchangeable instances of a single phenomenon. They are distinct cases with distinct evidence bases, distinct evolutionary hypotheses, and distinct ecological contexts. The Mapinguari, with its strong fossil lineage to the giant ground sloths and its position in the most biologically concealing habitat on Earth, is the most scientifically plausible of the three. Bigfoot, with the deepest evidence base and the most extensive investigation history, is the most thoroughly documented. The Yowie, with no fossil lineage support and no native primates on its continent, is the most challenging; the case that demands the most creative hypothesizing and that would produce the most revolutionary implications if confirmed. The comparative method has allowed each case to be seen more clearly by virtue of standing beside the others.

The space has been narrowed. The preceding chapters have systematically evaluated and, where appropriate, set aside the explanations that do not account for the full pattern: the misidentification hypothesis, which explains some encounters but not the core residual; the hoax hypothesis, which accounts for specific pieces of evidence but not the continental scope; the psychological hypothesis, which illuminates the perceptual filter but cannot generate the ecological calibration documented in the comparative data. What remains, after these filters have been applied, is smaller than the raw sighting database but more robust; a residual body of testimony that is too specific, too consistent, and too ecologically patterned to be comfortably dismissed by any single alternative explanation.

The space has been illuminated. The noise that surrounds the signal; the media contamination, the translation errors, the institutional barriers, the economic incentives, the digital amplification, has been mapped with enough specificity that future investigation can account for it rather than being consumed by it. The methodology for conducting a proper search has been described. The ecological feasibility of hidden populations has been modeled. The taxonomy for organizing cryptid claims has been proposed. The tools are in hand, even if the will to use them remains uncertain.

But the space has not been closed. The question remains open. And the final chapter of this book must reckon with what that openness means.

The Relict Hominoid Theory

There is a hypothesis that has circulated on the margins of mainstream science for more than half a century, never quite gaining acceptance but never quite going away. It is the idea that the hairy humanoids of global tradition: Bigfoot, the Yowie, the Yeti, and their many cousins are relict hominoids: surviving populations of a primate lineage that was once far more widespread than it is today, and that has persisted in isolated pockets of wilderness while the rest of the world moved on.

The framework for this theory is grounded in the fossil record. We know, with certainty, that the world was once home to a far greater diversity of large primates than exists today. *Gigantopithecus blacki*, an enormous ape that stood up to ten feet tall and inhabited the forests of Southeast Asia, survived until roughly three hundred thousand years ago; a blink of an eye in evolutionary terms. *Paranthropus*, a genus of robust, heavily built hominins, persisted in Africa until roughly one million years ago. The Denisovans, a branch of the human family tree only recently identified through genetic evidence, inhabited Asia and may have interbred with modern humans as recently as thirty thousand years ago. The world of the recent past was crowded with large, intelligent primates, and the idea that all of them went cleanly extinct; leaving no surviving remnant anywhere on the planet, is an assumption rather than a certainty.

The relict hominoid hypothesis proposes that some branch of this diverse primate family survived; perhaps *Gigantopithecus* in Asia, perhaps an unknown hominid lineage in the Americas, perhaps something else entirely in Australia, and that the creatures described in the global hairy humanoid traditions are the living descendants of these survivors. The mechanism of dispersal is the land bridges that connected the continents during the Pleistocene glaciations. The Bering Land Bridge, connecting Asia to North America during the last ice age, is the most commonly cited route for the hypothetical entry of a large primate into the New World. The chain of islands between Southeast Asia and Australia, crossed by human ancestors at least sixty thousand years ago, represents a more challenging but not impossible pathway for a second lineage.

In this book's terms, the relict hominoid hypothesis provides a parsimonious explanation for the Type I cases: the remarkable consistency of hairy humanoid descriptions across cultures and continents becomes the product of common ancestry, and the differences become the product of adaptive radiation; precisely the pattern of divergent adaptation documented in Chapter 5. The size gradient follows Bergmann's Rule because the creatures are real animals subject to real ecological pressures. The behavioral gradient follows habitat density because the creatures are real organisms responding to real spatial constraints. The smell, the vocalizations, the percussive communication, the nocturnal activity; all become the predictable features of a large, forest-dwelling, socially complex primate doing what primates do.

The hypothesis falters in two places. First, it does not accommodate the Mapinguari without modification. If the Mapinguari is a ground sloth descendant rather than a primate, it falls outside the relict hominoid framework; it is a different kind of survival, from a different lineage, requiring a different explanation. The global hairy humanoid phenomenon may not be a single phenomenon at all, but two or more distinct phenomena that have been conflated because their superficial similarities are more visible than their deep differences. This is precisely the kind of distinction that the taxonomy proposed in Chapter 15 is designed to preserve.

Second, the hypothesis cannot account for the complete absence of physical proof. If relict hominoid populations have been living and dying in these forests for millennia, the continued failure to recover a single confirmed specimen is a problem that the hypothesis must absorb rather than explain away. Chapter 6 demonstrated that the absence is less devastating than it initially appears: decomposition rates, fossil record bias, and detection probability mathematics all soften the blow, but the absence remains the central challenge, and no amount of ecological modeling eliminates it.

The relict hominoid theory remains unproven. But it remains, also, unfalsified. It stands as a framework; a way of organizing the available data into a coherent narrative that, while speculative, is grounded in established principles of biology, paleontology, and biogeography. Whether it will ever be confirmed or definitively disproven depends on evidence that has not yet been found.

The Archetype in the Forest

There is another way to read the global hairy humanoid phenomenon, and it begins not in the forest but in the deep structure of the human mind.

Carl Jung proposed the existence of archetypes: universal, inherited patterns of thought and imagery that reside in what he called the collective unconscious. These archetypes are not learned. They are not culturally transmitted in the conventional sense. They are, in Jung's model, part of the foundational architecture of the human psyche, as innate as the startle reflex, as universal as the capacity for language. Among the most powerful of these archetypes is the Wild Man; the figure of untamed, uncivilized humanity that exists outside the boundaries of social order. The Wild Man appears in the mythology of virtually every human culture across every era: Enkidu in the Sumerian Epic of Gilgamesh, the satyrs of Greek tradition, the woodwose of medieval European legend, the vanara of Hindu mythology, the green men of Celtic folklore. He is the part of ourselves that we have domesticated but not destroyed; the primal, animal core that civilization has suppressed but can never fully erase. The Jungian reading of the hairy humanoid phenomenon proposes that Bigfoot, the Mapinguari, and the Yowie are not biological entities but psychological ones; projections of the Wild Man archetype onto the landscape, given shape and substance by the deep human need to externalize the parts of ourselves that we cannot fully integrate. In this model, the creatures are real in a meaningful sense; they are real experiences, produced by a real cognitive mechanism, serving a real psychological function, but they are not flesh and blood. They are the shadow, in the Jungian sense: the dark, unacknowledged counterpart to the conscious, civilized self.

This interpretation has considerable explanatory power. It accounts for the global distribution of similar reports without requiring biological mechanisms of dispersal. It explains why the creatures are always found at the edges of civilization; because the archetype is, by definition, the thing that exists at the boundary between the known and the unknown self. It explains the emotional intensity of encounters; the primal fear, the sense of awe, the feeling of being in the presence of something ancient and fundamental because the archetype is, in Jung's framework, a direct encounter with the deepest layers of the psyche. But the Jungian reading, elegant as it is, encounters the same boundary that the psychological analysis of Chapter 8 encountered: it cannot account for the ecological calibration of the data. An archetype does not adjust its body size to Bergmann's Rule. A projection does not vary its territorial behavior with habitat pressure. A shadow does not leave footprints with dermal ridges, or produce vocalizations that register on a spectrograph, or generate a biological stench that precedes it through the forest and lingers after it has gone.

The archetype is part of the picture. The encounters resonate with such force partly because they touch something deep in the human psyche; something that recognizes the almost-human shape in the forest and responds with a dread that transcends the merely physical. But the archetype alone does not explain the data. And the data, imperfect and incomplete as it is, continues to include elements that resist reduction to psychology.

The Possibility That Both Are True

The most honest assessment: and the one that this book, after fifteen chapters of careful analysis, arrives at, is that the relict hominoid theory and the Jungian archetype are not mutually exclusive explanations. They may be two sides of the same ancient coin.

It is possible; perhaps even probable, that there is a real psychological phenomenon at work in the human response to the idea of the hairy humanoid. The Wild Man archetype, the HADD mechanism, the uncanny valley response, the deep-time predator circuitry; all of these contribute to an environment in which the human mind is primed to see, fear, and remember something large and almost-human in the forest. This psychological substrate generates some encounters that have no biological basis. It amplifies and distorts other encounters that may have a biological basis but that are filtered through a perceptual apparatus in crisis mode. It creates a cultural feedback loop in which media, community identity, and social reinforcement shape the testimony in ways that make the signal harder to extract.

But it is equally possible that this psychological substrate has been fed, over millennia, by encounters with something that is genuinely there.

Something that exists in the forests and the gorges and the deep places of the world. Something that is rare, intelligent, nocturnal, and evasive; and that, by the intersection of those qualities, has managed to coexist with human civilization for thousands of years without being captured, catalogued, and pinned down.

The two explanations do not cancel each other. They layer. The archetype provides the receptivity. The creature, if it exists, provides the stimulus. The encounter: the moment in the forest when something is seen, heard, smelled, and feared is the product of both, and the challenge of separating them is the challenge that defines the entire field.

The Unclosed Case

This book has been, from its first page, an exercise in honest uncertainty. It has not argued that these creatures exist. It has not argued that they do not. It has argued that the question is more complex, more interesting, and more resistant to easy resolution than either the believers or the skeptics typically acknowledge; and that the comparative method, applied with rigor and intellectual honesty, can reveal patterns in the data that single-case analysis cannot.

Those patterns have been documented. The convergent silhouette. The smell gradient. The behavioral gradient. The size gradient tracking with Bergmann's Rule. The foot morphologies calibrated to local substrate. The witness populations converging on experienced wilderness professionals with nothing to gain. The nocturnal activity pattern providing a coherent explanation for the photographic void. The ecological feasibility models leaving mathematical room for hidden populations in all three habitats.

And the patterns have been complicated. The noise of media contamination. The distortion of cultural translation. The gravitational pull of community identity. The institutional barriers that prevent the question from being asked by the people best equipped to answer it. The psychological substrate that primes the human observer to see exactly the kind of creature that is reported. The absence: the persistent, maddening, defining absence of the one piece of evidence that would settle it all.

Every year, new reports are filed. In the Pacific Northwest, hunters and hikers continue to describe encounters with something large and bipedal moving through the trees. In the Amazon, indigenous communities continue to speak of the thing that roars in the deep forest. In the Blue Mountains of Australia, bushwalkers continue to stumble onto something that should not be there. The witnesses are not, by and large, attention-seekers or the credulous. They are ordinary people who have had an extraordinary experience, and the consistency of their testimony across decades, continents, and cultures is a fact that resists comfortable explanation.

There is a tendency, in the modern world, to assume that everything has been discovered; that the age of exploration is over, that the map is complete, and that the blank spaces have all been filled in. This assumption is wrong. The oceans remain overwhelmingly unexplored. The tropical rainforests are still yielding new species at a remarkable rate. Even in the relatively well-studied forests of North America, new species of mammals have been identified in recent decades. The idea that a large, intelligent, deliberately elusive creature could remain undiscovered is not the fantasy it is often made out to be. It is a reflection of the simple, humbling reality that the world is larger and more complex than we tend to assume.

Country Cousins

The great hairy humanoids: Bigfoot, the Mapinguari, and the Yowie, may be real animals. They may be surviving relics of a more diverse primate past, pushed to the margins by the relentless expansion of our own species, holding on in the last wild places where the forest is deep enough to hide them. They may be archetypes: projections of the human psyche onto the landscape, serving a function as old as consciousness itself. They may be something that partakes of both realities, something that our current categories are not equipped to contain.

What they are not is settled. The file has not been closed. The verdict has not been reached.

And in the spaces between the trees, in the silence that falls over the bush when something large draws near, in the roar that echoes through the Amazon night, in the footprint pressed deep into the mud of a creek bed that no human foot could have made; the question remains. As alive and as unanswered as it has ever been.

These are our country cousins. We have not met them yet. But the introduction, it seems, is long overdue.

The next volume will bring three more to the table. The method will be the same. The creatures will be different. And the shadow at the edge of the firelight will shift; not closer, not farther, but into a new shape.

One root. Many branches. And the forest, as always, is not finished with us.

About the Author

K.M. Graves approaches the unexplained with a commitment to rigorous methodology, honest inquiry, and deep respect for both the people who experience unexplained phenomena and the locations that carry those stories. Their work sits at the intersection of investigative practice, human psychology, and the enduring mysteries that resist easy explanation. When not writing, they are usually researching case histories, historical records, or the precise line between what current science can measure and what it has not yet learned to ask.

K.M. Graves